T0285427

BIG
MEG

ALSO BY TIM FLANNERY

Mammals of New Guinea

Tree Kangaroos: A Curious Natural History with R. Martin, P. Schouten and A. Szalay

The Future Eaters

Possums of the World: a Monograph of the Phalangeroidea with P. Schouten

Mammals of the South West Pacific and Moluccan Islands

Watkin Tench, *1788* (ed.)

John Nicol, *Life and Adventures 1776–1801* (ed.)

Throwim Way Leg: An Adventure

The Explorers (ed.)

The Birth of Sydney (ed.)

Terra Australis: Matthew Flinders' Great Adventures in the Circumnavigation of Australia (ed.)

The Eternal Frontier

A Gap in Nature with P. Schouten

John Morgan, *The Life and Adventures of William Buckley* (ed.)

The Birth of Melbourne (ed.)

Joshua Slocum, *Sailing Alone around the World* (ed.)

Astonishing Animals with P. Schouten

Country

The Weather Makers

We Are the Weather Makers

An Explorer's Notebook

Here on Earth

Among the Islands

The Mystery of the Venus Island Fetish

Atmosphere of Hope

Sunlight and Seaweed

Europe

Life

The Climate Cure

TIM FLANNERY & EMMA FLANNERY

BIG MEG

The Story of the Largest and Most Mysterious Predator that Ever Lived

Atlantic Monthly Press

New York

First published in Australia in 2023 by the Text Publishing Company

Printed in the United States of America

First Grove Atlantic hardcover editon: February 2024

Typeset by J&M Typesetting

ISBN 978-0-8021-6258-8
eISBN 978-0-8021-6259-5

Library of Congress Cataloging-in-Publication data is available for this title.

Atlantic Monthly Press
an imprint of Grove Atlantic
154 West 14th Street
New York, NY 10011

Distributed by Publishers Group West

groveatlantic.com

24 25 26 27 28   10 9 8 7 6 5 4 3 2 1

Contents

To Dr Tom Rich, my lifelong mentor
TF

To my wonderful dad, for making this life
one of hope and adventure
EF

CHAPTER 1

The Discovery

When I was sixteen I found something that changed my life. It was 1973, the wettest year then recorded in Australia, and the desert heart of the continent was transformed into an inland sea. Cooper Creek and the Warburton River flowed like the Mississippi, and Lake Eyre, usually a vast dry salt pan, filled with freshwater, with pelicans and with other aquatic life. In my home state of Victoria, floods ripped through the landscape, carrying away soil and crops and livestock, leaving behind fields of debris and rubble. In those days I was a keen fossil hunter, and I knew that the floods might unearth hidden treasures last seen when Earth was a younger and different place.

My favourite fossil-hunting grounds were in western Victoria. There, the floods had been monumental and merciless, destroying houses, farms and sheds and carrying off countless flocks of sheep and herds of cattle. It was a bright summer day when I made my great discovery. The floods had subsided, leaving the creek I was prospecting scoured and filled with pebbly shoals. I was walking along the bank when I saw, in shallow water, a large, triangular shape nestled among the pebbles. I scampered down the slope and picked it up. As if in a dream, I realised that I was holding a huge tooth. I knew instantly what it was. I had read about such things, and even seen examples in museums. But I never dreamed that I'd be fortunate enough to find one. This tooth had once been in the mouth of a shark known as *Otodus megalodon*, the largest predator that ever lived, a mighty species that had been extinct for millions of years! The fossil was large enough to cover my palm. Its silken chestnut-brown enamel shone brilliantly in the sunshine. So magical did it appear that I handled it gently, not daring to put it down in case it disappeared.

Years later when I visited that creek, I discovered the partial skeleton of a whale eroding from the bank just upstream from where I made my find. I knew that the megalodon preyed on whales, and I suspect that the flood had ripped my tooth from the sediment around the skeleton, where it had been dropped as the shark tore into its prey. Courtesy of volcanic activity, which had elevated the entire region, the site was now well inland—a hundred kilometres from the sea. It was dizzying to think that 10 million years ago the largest predator ever to exist had swum where I then walked.

I still have that great tooth. It's my talisman of time travel and one of my most treasured possessions. I've spent countless hours, tracing its fate from the moment it fell from the shark's mouth to the moment, half a century ago, when I spotted it in the creek bed. In my mind's eye I see the tooth tumbling from the shark's mouth as it crunched down on the carcass of the whale, before sashaying through the water and falling to the bottom. A rain of sandy sediment, mostly formed from the bodies of dead sea creatures, buried it many metres deep. Millions of years later a volcano spewed out a lava flow, sealing its stony tomb. Groundwater carried phosphate and other minerals from the sediment into the enamel of the tooth, staining it a rich chestnut brown. Eventually volcanism elevated the rocks, and a drying climate created the characteristic woodlands of the volcanic plains in Victoria's Western District. In time, a creek cut into the land, first eroding through the lava, then cutting into the sediments that held the fossil. The most subtle of topographic variation must have guided the creek as it excavated its valley ever deeper into the rock, until by pure fluke it cut into the sediment where the tooth lay. In 1973 a raging flood unearthed the fossil, exposing it to daylight for the first time in 10 million years, damaging it slightly in the process, and deposited it on the pebble bank where I found it. The chances of me ever encountering that megalodon tooth are so fantastically small that it has come to symbolise, for me, immense good fortune.

A couple of years after I made that find I finished high school. I was then nearly eighteen, and a long summer holiday beckoned. Most of my mates would spend it surfing or chasing girls. But I was going to hunt fossils, mostly by snorkelling or scuba-diving off a rocky beach at Beaumaris, a few kilometres from my home in suburban Melbourne. The fossil deposits there, which are around six million years old, crop out on the bed of Port Phillip Bay in a few metres of water. I had stumbled across them a decade earlier, when I was eight, and over the years had found hundreds of fossilised sharks' teeth there, as well as the bones of many other kinds of extinct marine creatures. I used to bring them to the curator of fossils at the Museum of Victoria, Dr Tom Rich, who hoped that I'd find remains from smaller mammals, such as seals or marsupials whose carcasses had been swept out to sea and become buried in the sediments.

Tom became one of the most important people in my life. He saw that I had the potential to become a palaeontologist and encouraged me to pursue higher studies. He also took me on field trips to remote regions of Australia, where he showed me the art of palaeontology—everything from how to encase a delicate fossil in a plaster jacket to how to sort and identify fossils. These are skills you don't learn in the classroom. They can only be acquired through a sort of apprenticeship, and I became Tom's eager apprentice. Perhaps the most important lesson he taught me was patience. 'You have to have the will to fail' he'd say to me whenever the fossils became thin on the ground and I started to lose interest.

One of the most important discoveries I had made at Beaumaris was the articulated backbone of an extinct seal. It was then the oldest seal fossil ever found in Australia, and Tom reckoned that the rest of the skeleton must be out there somewhere. Indeed, so convinced was he that he offered to pay me the then princely sum of $500 to search for it over that summer. I was delighted to take up Tom's offer. In fact I would gladly have spent the summer diving at Beaumaris without any pay. Apart from being a mad-keen fossil hunter, I loved exploring the marine environment with its many species of fish and starfish and other invertebrates. The only stipulation Tom made on the deal was that I must hand over every fossil I found, whether of a seal or any other creature.

On my very first day on the job—in fact just a few minutes after I had slipped into the shallows—I saw, lying before me on the sea floor, a perfect megalodon tooth. It

was even larger than my first find, and it was more complete. Its enamel was lustrous, glossy green in colour, and
as I floated in the sunny water above it shone from its bed
of sand with an uncanny brilliance. I'd been scanning that
area for years, and must have swum right over it dozens of
times. But now a current had washed some sand away, or
perhaps a storm had dislodged a stone that had obscured
the great tooth, and there it lay in all its beauty, like an
expensive necklace in a jeweller's window.

I dived down, picked it up, and placed it in the linen
bag I carried for my finds. I took it home and put it on
the shelf in my bedroom with my other treasures, which
included a fossilised whale vertebra and the teeth of lesser
sharks. Like a prince among paupers, it outshone them
all. That evening I lay in bed, admiring it, and struggling
with a moral dilemma of monumental proportions. Under
the terms of my agreement, the tooth belonged to Tom
Rich and the museum. But nobody would know if I kept
it. I could always say that I had found it before or after
my period of employment. The trouble with that idea was
that I would know. That night, as I struggled with what to
do, I dreamed of walking over beaches paved with perfect
megalodon teeth. So many that I could not pick them all
up. When I awoke, overcome with a special kind of sadness
I'd never known before or since, I knew what I had to do.

I'd board the train to the city, and hand my megalodon tooth over to Dr Rich. It could, I realised, be mine only for this one night.

I arrived at the museum as self-importantly as if I were bearing the Rosetta Stone or the Nefertiti bust and was expecting gasps of astonishment or whoops of joy from Dr Rich. But when I revealed my treasure, Tom barely noticed. I was wounded at the casual way he took the tooth from my hands, as if it were a mere trinket. Dr Rich, I had forgotten, was not interested in the fossils of sharks. He wanted fossils of seals. In a teenage mood somewhere between crestfallen and resentful, I stomped away.

From the moment I left Dr Rich's office that morning, I didn't see that tooth again for more than 40 years. Yet it filled my daydreams, and my dreams. My university textbooks became filled with doodles of fossil shark teeth, and in my dreams I often found myself walking along a sea wall, above dozens of fossilised megalodon teeth, so many that they spilled from my hands. I would invariably wake up after such dreams feeling happy and wealthy beyond measure.

On my fiftieth birthday, I decided to give myself a present. I was then director of the South Australian Museum whose shop had a few megalodon teeth from North America. I purchased one that had been found in a river in South

Carolina. It cost me $1500, and I valued it. But it could never, at least in my mind, be as significant as the tooth I had found all those years ago.

Over the years Tom and I have remained very close, and I often visited him at the Museum of Victoria. But it was not until 2019 that I asked to see the beautiful megalodon tooth I'd handed over 41 years earlier. I don't know why it took me so long to muster the will to do so. But I felt a compulsion to know whether the great tooth was as large and glorious in reality as it was in my memory. A good friend, Dr Erich Fitzgerald, was by that time the curator in charge of marine vertebrate fossils at the museum. He took me into the collection and opened a drawer filled with the teeth of megalodon sharks found at Beaumaris. Most had been collected during the 19th Century, when the sea floor must have been littered with such treasures, just as it was in my dreams.

The fossil bed at Beaumaris has been eroding away for thousands of years, exposing a rich variety of fossil bones and teeth. The fossils are far harder than the stone that encloses them and can be so abundant as to form a kind of pavement of bones, stones and other remnants. During the ice ages the waters of Port Phillip Bay drained away and the place was a plain. Back then, during the freezing days and nights, the fossils must have lain among the roots of grasses and snow gums and been trod on by diprotodons and other giant marsupials. When the Earth warmed and the waters rose, the fossils once more became part of the bed of a shallow sea, and waves ground them against one another, smoothing their sharp cutting edges. Many of the megalodon teeth Erich showed me had become so worn by the waves that they looked more like shiny pebbles than the razor-sharp teeth of a giant predator.

We examined box after box containing megalodon teeth, and drawer after drawer. Eventually Erich began to look worried. He had to admit it: my megalodon tooth could not be found. Had it been stolen, I wondered? Erich admitted that, despite the vigilance of staff, such beautiful fossils occasionally went missing from museums all around the world. Erich's words left me feeling downcast. It was as if I had lost some precious part of myself.

After the fruitless search I dropped into Tom Rich's office to say hello. By then in his late seventies, Tom was almost blind, and he sat in his darkened office in front of a computer screen that bathed him in a ghostly light. I told him the dismal news and he said that he had entirely forgotten about the tooth. After a thoughtful pause he airily added, 'I would have been happy for you to keep it. All I wanted were the fossils of seals and land-mammals. You should have just asked.'

Thunderstruck, I stalked away, vexed at myself and the world. But then, a few weeks later, Erich called me.

He had kept searching the collections after I had left and had found my megalodon tooth. It had been misfiled— placed in the wrong drawer. The next day I rushed into the museum, my heart full of anticipation. Erich met me in his office, the tooth cradled in his hand just as I had once cradled it. He handed it to me, and I beheld the fossil. It was just as lustrous and glorious in reality as it was in my memory.

The sensation of holding the fossil again had a magical effect on me. I realised that I no longer needed to own it. Instead, I saw that it was a unique piece of history: my history, Victorian history and world history. And, despite having been misplaced, it was far safer in the museum than it would have been in my home. In the museum it forms part of the great narrative story of evolution in Australia and is available for study by one and all. And I can visit it whenever I like, heft it, and recall the day I discovered it. I think I had finally grown up.

CHAPTER 2

The Megalodon

Imagine an enormous predatory shark weighing 60,000 kilograms—twice as much as a humpback whale. Just ponder that for a moment. The shark is making its way through coastal waters off Africa: its body moving to a tonic rhythm, as if to a beating drum; its scythe-like fin, taller than a man, parting the waves. *Otodus megalodon* is the largest predator ever to exist, and this one can scent a pod of baleen whales, one of which is injured. The great shark, which is many times the size of any of these whales, approaches from behind and brutally attacks the injured one, forcing the healthy whales to flee. The megalodon is businesslike in its butchering, slicing off the injured whale's tail flukes with a single bite of its two-metre-wide jaws, then severing the creature's pectoral fins, leaving it helpless. Like most predators it's careful not to get injured as it attacks. There is then a moment of quiet as it leaves the terrified and agonised whale bleeding and entirely helpless in the water until merciful death takes it.

A distant human ancestor, an *Australopithecus*, watches the drama from a nearby bluff. Fascinated by the attack, it stores away details that might be useful if it ever finds itself vulnerable in the sea. As our ancestor watches, the megalodon launches itself at the carcass from below, tossing the mutilated body many metres into the air, disembowelling it at a stroke. The predator then sets to work dismembering the corpse, bite by bite, swallowing hunks of flesh metres across and weighing tonnes. In the swirling, bloodstained waters, lesser sharks cruise, seeking scraps.

Such a scene is likely to have been witnessed many times by our ancestors, and it doubtless inspired both fear and awe. But then, one day, the last megalodon died. Firsthand knowledge of its behaviour would be lost forever. The megalodon would become known only from its fossilised teeth, and a few vertebrae. But the impression the living beast made on our ancestors' psyches surely joined that of myriad other long-lost predators, spawning nebulous fears of monsters as varied as dragons, krakens,

Grendels, zombies and, with Hollywood, merciless gigantic sharks.

Over the history of our human lineage, the prospect of being eaten alive has been a very real possibility. And it has left us with a morbid fascination—a hardwired need to observe closely the gory attacks of predators, to learn from them. Think of the millions of years during which our ancestors survived without even a fire to protect themselves. The only defence against being eaten at night by a leopard was to climb into inaccessible perches among rocks and trees and to shiver there in the cold, remaining aware enough to see the gleam of the approaching eye, or to hear the muffled rasp of its breath. Terror, and anxiety that never fully abates, the ability to survive sleepless night after sleepless night, these are the sieves through which evolution selected 'the fittest' of our ancestors over countless millennia. And the consequences of that sieving—including baseless anxiety—are still with us. Evolution doesn't care for our comfort. It doesn't care whether, from cradle to grave, we are plagued by nightmares and nameless terrors, or that our imaginings are filled with the most gruesome of monsters. Our evolved psyches don't know that most of the human-eating monsters are now gone from our world, and that constant vigilance against the terrors of the night are no longer a prerequisite for survival. So embedded indeed are those monsters in our minds that we compulsively resurrect them in stories, books and movies—even those like the megalodon that have been gone for millions of years. Only evolution through natural selection that favours the less-anxious mind could do away with the monsters that haunt our dreams. But in a world of wars, with its ever-present dangers of senseless assault and rape, we are our own monsters. And that makes the future evolution of a less-anxious mind a distant prospect indeed.

The megalodon, aka *Otodus megalodon*, the big meg, is the largest predator that has ever existed. Conservative estimates put its weight at 50 tonnes, while some suggest 100 tonnes. That's more than half the weight of an adult blue whale. And this leviathan of a predator was warm-blooded. Such a stupendous creature is impossible in today's world. The largest great white sharks alive today weigh a mere two tonnes, the largest orcas just over six. Either would be just a snack for the megalodon, providing enough sustenance, perhaps, for a few days or weeks. The megalodon was in fact so outsized that its mere existence has forced us to rethink the nature of the oceans it swam in, and to ask why our modern world is so diminished. Moreover, recent discoveries have revealed scarcely believable aspects of its behaviour that further deepen the enigma of its existence.

There is no doubt that the megalodon was a ferocious predator. Computer models reveal the force of its bite to be a whopping 100,000–180,000 newtons, by far the most

powerful bite of any animal that has ever existed. It is fourteen times greater than the bite force of the great white
shark, and 83–138 times greater than that of humans. By
comparison, *Tyrannosaurus rex* could bite with a force of
64,000 newtons—which is enough, indeed, to crush a car,
Jurassic Park style. But a bite of 100,000–180,000 newtons
would not just crush a car but dismember it—possibly
atomise it. Why would any creature require such a forceful bite? After all, great white sharks can tear apart the
carcasses of whales perfectly adequately with their relatively
feeble bite force. What prey could possibly require such
power? The jaws that bit with such force also had a prodigious, metres-wide gape—tooth-studded arches sufficient
to swallow an orca whole. The largest megalodon tooth
ever found measures eighteen centimetres from base to tip
and weighs about 1.5 kilograms. That's longer than the
teeth of any marine predator living today, except perhaps
the largest sperm whales. It almost certainly came from an
individual that exceeded 15 metres in length.

The megalodon is no relic of deep time. It survived
until relatively recently, geologically speaking, living far
more recently than the dinosaurs which vanished about
66 million years ago. Megalodon evolved from somewhat
smaller, but still very large shark ancestors some 40 million
years after the last dinosaur died. This is about the time
that the first apes evolved in Africa, so our lineage shares a

similar time span with the megalodon. And the megalodon
became extinct only 4.5–2.5 million years ago as the Earth
was cooling towards the ice ages. As it vanished, another
super-predator, the bipedal apes of our own genus, which
would eventually give rise to *Homo sapiens*, were taking
form. It must be said, however, that a few people, known as
cryptozoologists, believe that the great shark never became
extinct. They think that it continues to lurk in the deepest parts of the ocean, a rarely glimpsed and poorly documented phantom killer of the abyss. Many cryptozoologists
believe that the Himalayan Yeti and North American Big
Foot too are real. We shall examine the evidence they mar-
shal in due course. But first we must get to know the megalodon itself.

Despite its immense size, and the profound impact the
megalodon must have had on the ecosystems of its day, the
species remains largely a mystery. We know much less about
it, for example, than we know about most of the dinosaurs.
We do not know for sure exactly how long it was, pre-
cisely how much it weighed or what shape it was for the
simple reason that cartilage, which comprises a shark's
skeleton, does not fossilise readily, and to date no complete
body fossil of the megalodon has ever been found. I often
curse the evolutionary twist that left sharks boneless and
so created this gap on the fossil record. Imagine if all we
knew about *Tyrannosaurus rex*, or the sabre-tooth cat, was

a few vertebrae and random piles of disassociated teeth?
Admittedly, many extinct species were once known from
similarly meagre fragments, but year by year palaeontologists have discovered more of their remains, allowing us to
have a much more realistic picture of these vanished species.
In the case of the megalodon, more complete fossils have
been very slow to appear. But advances are being made.
To adapt the maxim of Jean Anthelme Brillat-Savarin: all
species are what they eat, and that shows up in the chemical isotopes stored in their bones and teeth. The applica-
tion of new technology to the fragmentary fossils that have
been collected is providing information about stunning and
unexpected aspects of the megalodon's biology and ecology.
Even a more accurate estimate of the time of its extinction
may one day be determined by isotopic analyses.

While the new frontier of biochemical palaeontology
has yielded exciting finds, there are fundamental ques-
tions that can only be answered by the recovery of more
complete fossils, and if we wish to know the megalodon,
we must first turn to these. The chances of any individual
creature leaving a fossil must be a billion to one, and the
chances of leaving a complete body fossil are far slimmer.
But palaeontologists and fossil hunters continue to hope
that a complete body fossil of the megalodon will one
day emerge from the rocks. Such hopes are not entirely
unrealistic. Complete and near-complete body fossils of

other kinds of sharks are occasionally unearthed. Finding an entire megalodon body fossil would be one of the great moments in palaeontology—a once-in-a-century discovery that would clarify in an instant our murky imaginings of the beast.

By far the most common fossil finds of the megalodon are teeth. These fossil teeth can be enormous, and their size and shape establishes that the megalodon was a member of an extinct lineage of sharks known as the megatooth sharks. Almost all of the fossil teeth of the megalodon are found as isolated specimens. This is due to the fact that sharks continually shed their teeth. Over their lives they produce many thousands of teeth, although just a few hundred are present in the mouth at any one time. The continuous replacement of worn and damaged sharks' teeth can occur because there is a sort of conveyor belt consisting of teeth at various stages of development in the mouth of every shark. The dental conveyor belt is known as a tooth stack, and usually four teeth are present in each stack, the foremost and oldest the one in use, while three teeth in various stages of development lie behind it. Continuous replacement ensures that sharks have dentitions that are always full of razor-sharp teeth. It also accounts for the fact that shark's teeth are among the most abundant of all vertebrate fossils.

It is exceedingly rare to find an associated set of teeth of any kind of shark, for this can only result from the death of an individual and the sinking of its carcass in very still waters where sediments can build up and cover the teeth before they are scattered. Even in such circumstances, however, the teeth tend to fall from the rotting carcass and although they can stay in proximity, their relationship to each other (as they were in the shark's mouth) is lost.

The most complete partial set of teeth of the megalo- don ever found comes from middle Miocene sediments in Japan, but even these teeth were found in a jumbled pile, with some missing. Using such finds, and other less- complete sets of teeth, scientists have reconstructed the order in which the teeth of the megalodon occurred in its jaws. They have been aided in their work by the discovery of three partial sets of teeth of a direct ancestor of the meg- alodon, known as *Otodus angustidens,* which lived about 30 million years ago. One of these partial sets was unearthed in 2018, by schoolteacher Philip Mullaly, on the southern coast of Victoria. Philip was on the hunt for fossils near a popular surfing beach known as Jan Juc when he saw a shiny, serrated tooth protruding from a rock that had fallen from the cliffs. Excited, he contacted Museum Victoria and it was not long before a team of scientists descended on the site and recovered forty additional teeth. All are most likely from the same individual, which in life would have had hundreds in its mouth. As they excavated the block, the palaeontologists came across several fossil teeth from sixgill sharks intermixed with those of the ancestral megalodon. Sixgill sharks, which still exist off the coast of Victoria today, are avid scavengers that often feed off the carcasses of whales, sharks and other oceanic creatures, losing the odd tooth in the process. It seems likely that after the *Otodus angustidens* died, the decaying, foetid corpse attracted scavengers, including the sixgills.

The discovery of a complete set of teeth of the megalodon, preserved in life position, would revolutionise our understanding of the creature. Complete dentitions, in life position, of many other shark species have been found, and perhaps it's only a matter of time before a complete dentition of a megalodon in life position is located. When it is, we will learn more details about how its awesome jaws worked, and will perhaps be able to shed more light on its preferred prey. But for now, a few piles of randomly dropped teeth which we assume come from a single individual, are the only direct evidence we have to guess how many teeth the great shark had in its head, and how they were arranged.

If the discovery of a complete set of teeth in life position excites the imagination, just think of what a full body fossil of the megalodon might yield! We might finally see how long and stiff its fins were, what its skin and cranium were like, and we'd have proof of the creature's true size. Perhaps its stomach contents would provide evidence of its prey. Maybe we would even see some details of the eye, including its size and position, along with any sculpturing patterns of its body that helped streamline it, enhancing its speed and agility.

Such a discovery is possible. In 2011 scientists published research describing the partial skeleton of a six-million-year-old fossilised ancestor of the great white shark. It consisted of a beautifully preserved set of jaws, complete with teeth in life position, and 45 vertebrae of an individual estimated to have been about five metres long. A Peruvian olive farmer stumbled on this spectacular fossil in 1988, and thankfully recognised its importance. It was purchased by Dr Gordon Hubbell, a famous collector of fossil shark teeth. The ancestral great white shark fossil was described by Dana J. Ehret, who named it *Carcharodon hubbelli* in honour of the avid shark-tooth collector who had established a private collection in Gainesville, Florida, which contains over one million specimens.

Dr Hubbell trained and worked as a vet, and eventually became a zoo director. He was an avid fisherman, and spent a decade fishing for sharks in Miami, dissecting, studying and sometimes eating his catch. In his home there is a room jammed with shark jaws: they cover every wall, and include a set from the largest great white shark ever accurately measured (it was almost six metres long). When a friend suggested he try his luck hunting for fossilised shark teeth in a locality in central Florida he was 'bitten by the shark-tooth bug' as he put it. At his fossil-hunting peak, Hubbell was collecting a thousand teeth a day.

Although it is hard to imagine, what is today a desert landscape in Peru was once an ocean bustling with a bio-logical richness far greater than any that currently exists. Six million years ago, in what is known today as the Pisco Formation, Hubbell's shark and the megalodon swam in the same ocean. Did they compete for food, or interact in other ways? It's tempting to think so, but without further research we can't know for sure.

If I were to dedicate my life to finding the body fossil of a megalodon, I'd start in the Pisco Formation, with its beautiful desert scenery and complete skeletons of whales lying exposed like shipwrecks in the sands. It's a stark land where the ancient sea floor, miraculously preserved, is laid out in exquisite detail. I'd wander those arid plains with their mirages, dust and the debris of a long-vanished sea. It would be like wandering through time itself. And imagine, just imagine, seeing the tip of a great tooth standing proud in the dust, the glint of its enamel in the bright sunlight catching the eye. And to dig, revealing more and more teeth in serried rows. After days of effort moving metres of rock, the rounded shape of the first vertebra might appear, and eventually the long triangle of a fin. For a fleeting moment

I'd be the only person on Earth to know the dimensions of the greatest predator that ever lived.

If a body fossil of the megalodon is ever found in the Pisco Formation, it may even retain remnants of its last meal. In 2017 a breathtaking discovery made there was reported: the body fossil of the giant mackerel shark, *Carcharodon hastalis*, replete with fish in its belly. The fossil, which is between 5 and 11 million years old, is so well preserved that the cartilage composing the shark's jaw is still visible. Along with the remains of pilchard bones in its stomach are piles of scales, suggesting that its final meal was at least partially digested at the time it died. The Pisco Formation is an example of a Fossil-Lagerstätte—an area of exceptional fossil preservation. Fossil-Lagerstätten can develop in several ways, but most often they form as a result of high sedimentation rates, rapid burial and a low oxygen content in the water, all of which hinder scavenging and decomposition. The spectacular preservation seen in the Pisco Formation has been enhanced by factors triggered when the remains were already buried in sediment. The partial decomposition of organic matter resulted in a loss of oxygen in the sediment, facilitating the development of rocky concretions that encased the remains, which protected them when they were exposed at the surface.

In the very rarest of circumstances a shark fossil is so
well preserved that we can discern the brain, muscles and
even claspers (the male shark's mating organ), as was the
case for a young school shark (*Galeorhinus cuvieri*) that was
scientifically described in 2016. Moments before its death
and its journey towards the anoxic sea floor, it had consumed a barracuda whose undigested skeleton can still be
seen in the region of the shark's stomach. So extraordinary
is its preservation that its dark fin tips can even be made
out. This incredible fossil is 50 million years old. It was
encased in a slab of rock retrieved from the Monte Bolca
Lagerstätte in northern Italy. The rocks around Molte
Bolca have also yielded the exceptionally preserved fossils of
many species of fish which are characteristic of types inhab-
iting coral reefs today. These fossils provide evidence of one
of the earliest known assemblages of coral-reef organisms,
supporting the idea that the region, which today forms
the foothills of the Italian Alps, was once a warm, shallow lagoon inshore of one of the world's earliest coral reefs.
Interestingly, the slab of stone containing the reef shark also
contained several less-well-preserved juvenile school sharks,
indicating that the lagoon may have served as a shark nursery, as many tropical reef lagoons do today.

Apart from a few piles of disarticulated teeth, the most
important fossils of the megalodon found to date are vertebrae, which are occasionally preserved due to a fluke of

geochemistry. While it's generally believed that a shark's skeleton is entirely made up of cartilage, large parts of it are in fact lightly calcified, the soft cartilage being coated with a layer of tiny calcite crystals held together by collagen. When a shark dies, the organic collagen swiftly degrades, and the calcite crystals fall apart. But the central part of some shark vertebrae is composed of a particular kind of calcified cartilage that is more resistant to decomposition than cartilage elsewhere, and so has a better chance of becoming fossilised.

As a shark swims, almost all the strain on its skeleton is absorbed by its vertebral column, which acts like a powerful spring, conserving energy for use with the next flexing. Amazingly, the vertebrae of sharks are stronger than those of cows. As a shark grows, the cartilage in its vertebrae is laid down in concentric rings, causing the bones to increase in diameter. This ring-like growth pattern, which is a little like the growth rings of trees, allows scientists to determine the shark's rate of growth and its age at the time of death.

In 2021, the 15-million-year-old vertebral column of a megalodon was subjected to analysis using advanced techniques. Discovered in the 1860s in Belgium, the fossil is the most complete set of vertebrae of the megalodon ever found. At the time of its discovery palaeontology was a very new science, and it is fortunate indeed that the specimen was collected at all. For 160 years it lay in the storehouse of the Royal Belgian Institute of Natural Sciences in Brussels, and generations of museum administrators and curators doubtless cursed the bulky rocks for taking up so much space. Thank heavens they were not disposed of (as many such museum fossils have been over the years) and that they survived the wars, economic hardship and various space-saving initiatives that were the lot of European museums through the 20th Century.

During the Covid-19 pandemic, shark-fossil expert Kenshu Shimada wrote to his colleague Matthew Bonnan at Stockton University in the US about micro-CT scans of the vertebrae. These 3D images permitted the researchers to look inside the vertebrae slice by slice, without needing to travel. Extraordinary revelations followed. The largest of the 150 disarticulated vertebrae is 15.5 centimetres wide, and the micro-CT scanner allowed the scientists to count the growth bands in the bone. They found that the bands were formed in pairs, one narrow and one wide, with the pairs laid down on a yearly basis. Presumably the wide one marks a season of plenty, and the narrow one a lean time. By studying these growth bands scientists estimated that the shark was 46 years old when it died, and that it had reached a length of about nine metres. A conservative extrapolation drawn from these observations suggests that megalodons could live for up to a hundred years, and that they could grow at a rate of 16 centimetres a year for the first half of their lives. By the standards of most living sharks, that makes the megalodon a slow-growing and long-lived animal. Intriguingly the researchers were also able to establish that when new-born, these sharks were more than two metres long, making them the largest sharks at birth ever known.

Among sharks, large pups are indicative of both live birth and an unsavoury behaviour known as intrauterine cannibalism. This behaviour occurs in species of sharks that don't have a placenta, and without a placenta it's impossible for mother sharks to get enough nutrients to their offspring while they are in the womb, to enable them to be born at a viable size. Intrauterine cannibalism involves the strongest of the unborn shark siblings that share their mothers' uteri (sharks, unlike humans, have two uteri) eating the others. Sharks that practise intrauterine cannibalism produce very large eggs, which hatch internally. In the most benign instances the behaviour takes the form of the mother continuing to release eggs into her uteri, which are then consumed by her first-born developing young. But the growing embryos can also attack and consume other embryos in the uteri. Taken to its logical extreme, intrauterine cannibalism results in just one young shark being born from each uterus—a small litter size indeed. The behaviour has evolved because even though only one or a few baby sharks survive in species that practise it, they will be healthier and larger at birth than they would have been if they hadn't eaten their siblings, and so have a better chance of survival than the progeny from a large litter of smaller sharks.

One feature that may be associated with intrauterine cannibalism is an elevated body temperature. This occurs in part because the female has high energy requirements resulting from the need to produce the surplus young and eggs. An elevated body temperature allows for more active foraging, during which more food can be obtained, so a positive feedback loop is created. Isotopic analysis of fossil tooth enamel shows the megalodon may have had a body temperature of 35–40°C. This is comparable with whales, and indeed with humans, and is much higher than that of any other shark. Perhaps the enormous bulk of the great shark helped it maintain such a high body temperature. Whatever the case, it adds to our knowledge of how the megalodon may have behaved. Perhaps it was continually active, as are orcas, and able to venture, at least temporarily, into cool waters and actively forage there.

Studies of both the fossil teeth and vertebrae of the megalodon suggest that individuals grew from more than two metres long at birth to at least 15 metres long in adult-hood. Humans and many other mammals go through much lesser changes in size from birth to adulthood, and because the young can be fed on milk, while they suckle they can be thought of as occupying the same ecological niche as their mothers. Sharks, however, experience large shifts in habitat and ecology as they grow. Young great white sharks, for example, start out as fish eaters in relatively warm waters, and as they grow they move into cooler waters where they eat seals. The very largest then specialise in scavenging whale carcasses. The very largest of megalodons might have been up to 20 metres long (though this is widely disputed)—more than triple the length of the largest great white shark, leading some researchers to think that they experienced even more varied shifts in ecology throughout their lives. It's difficult to imagine what such leviathans fed on, but their diet could have been very different from that which sustained individuals half their length.

Many sharks use breeding grounds, which are often shallow, partially enclosed coastal areas that act as nurseries, both protecting pups from predation and providing an abundant supply of suitable food. Some living shark species, such as the bull shark, for example, give birth in protected estuaries where the less salty water deters potential predators, and there are abundant estuary fish for the young to feed on. There is some evidence that megatooth sharks used nursery areas. Nursery grounds used by the megalodon's direct ancestor *Otodus angustidens* have been identified in eastern North America. Almost 90 per cent of *O. angustidens* fossil teeth collected from a site near Summerville, South Carolina, were shown to be juveniles. The site was a rarity in that it was undisturbed by amateur fossil collectors, an important factor when doing population studies, as the preferential collection of larger teeth by amateur fossil hunters can skew data. The locality was once a shallow marine ecosystem replete with fish, sea turtles, dolphins and small cetaceans, perfect hunting grounds for young *O. angustidens*.

There is some evidence that megalodons used specific nursery grounds, returning again and again to the same areas to give birth. In fossil deposits derived from these localities, juvenile teeth occur in abundance, and the teeth of large adults are rare. One study published in 2020 identified only five such nursery areas globally. One is in the Tarragona Basin, Spain, a second at Calvert Cliffs, Maryland, a third in Bone Valley, Florida, with a final two areas (the Gatún and Chucunaque Formations) in Panama. It thus seems possible that nursery grounds suitable for the megalodon were highly restricted. For the young sharks to survive, these areas must have provided abundant food resources (perhaps fish for the youngest sharks), allowing the pups to grow quickly. In young megalodons, the teeth of the lower jaw tend to narrow rapidly from their base. The teeth of the giant mackerel shark, *Carcharodon hastalis*, which was a fish eater, are similar in shape. They may have served a rather similar function to the spikes on a steak board—to hold the slippery food in place, as the upper teeth act like steak knives to saw through it. If this is correct, it may be that the diet of young megalodons included fish. Nursery grounds must have excluded most larger sharks and other predators which could have fed on the pups. As yet, no full analysis of the wider geological context, sediments and fauna is available for any of the megalodon's nursery grounds, so we know little about the specific conditions in which its young were nurtured.

One particular avenue of study should be a priority. Except for the fact that the lower teeth of very young megalodons narrow sharply towards their apex, most juvenile megalodon teeth are shaped much like those of the adults. But many of the smallest fossil megalodon teeth unearthed from the Bone Valley Formation are heart-shaped. This unusual shape is due to the short, broad tooth crowns and the contour of the roots. These teeth are often referred to as 'Hubbell teeth', after Dr Gordon Hubbell, who first recognised them. There is some speculation that Hubbell teeth are the teeth that a megalodon was born with. It is also possible, however, that they result from some other cause, such as a nutrient deficiency—though this does not explain why only the smallest teeth are so shaped. These fossils are so far rather understudied. If they are indeed the teeth that the megalodon was born with, their occurrence may be a useful guide for distinguishing birthing grounds, as opposed to areas merely frequented by young sharks.

One danger to newborn megalodons may have been the presence of other shark species, such as *Carcharodon hubbelli*, the ancient relative of the great white shark, whose teeth are found in some nursery grounds that scientists have identified as being used by megalodons. We know from the analysis of fossilised vertebrae that the growth rate of young megalodons was even faster than that of *C. hubbelli*. This rapid growth may have allowed young megalodons to protect themselves from such predators, by permitting them to quickly migrate to deeper waters, where predators may have been fewer, and where food sources suitable for larger individuals occurred.

Most reconstructions of the megalodon have used the great white shark as a model. But sharks have evolved to exploit many ways of being top predators, and some of the strangest may offer new ways of imagining the megalodon. Of all the many species of large sharks alive today, surely the most bizarre and, indeed, horrific is the Greenland shark. A predator of the frozen waters of the Arctic Ocean and deep sea, it can grow to seven metres in length, making it one of the largest of living shark species—capable of swallowing a seal or a reindeer whole. But rather than the sleek, fast terror of the great white shark, the Greenland shark is more of a deep-sea zombie. Except when ambushing prey (when it is lightning fast with its bite) it is eerily slow, moving at speeds of just over one kilometre per hour.

This makes it the slowest fish in the ocean for its size. You could easily outswim a Greenland shark—at least for a while. But the thing about the zombie shark is that it never tires. It will just keep tracking its prey until the hunted animal takes a rest. Then it makes that lightning-fast lunge.

Greenland sharks can look rotted—the skin of some is covered in patches of green algae-like matter with irregular black and pale areas, and their fins can appear stumpy and sometimes ragged. One observer in the 1840s noted that the body of one Greenland shark continued to twitch for three days after its head was cut off, and that if a man were to put his hand into the mouth of its severed head, it would be bitten off. The Greenland shark is not only hard to kill, but slow to develop. Gestation can take between eight and eighteen years. After being born, it can live seemingly forever. One Methuselah, whose age was estimated to be at least 272 years, is the current record holder. But some researchers assert that individuals of the species can probably live for more than 400 years.

Perhaps the most horrifying thing about the Greenland shark is its eyes. If you look at a photograph of one, you might see two strands, like thick spaghetti, extending from the eye sockets. These strands are worm-like parasitic crustaceans, each up to three centimetres long, which live by eating out the shark's corneas, leaving their long, filamentous bodies trailing from the sightless eye sockets.

In the sub-zero, total darkness of waters up to 2200 metres deep that the Greenland shark favours, it has little need for vision. Instead, it finds its prey by blindly following scent trails, relentlessly tracking a carcass, injured animal, or other prey—until it has its day.

In Arctic waters, Greenland sharks can come into shallower waters to feed, and there they can encounter terrestrial species. The remains of a polar bear has been found in the gut of one, as have the bones of caribou (as reindeer are known in North America). Whether these meals resulted from attacks on living animals, or from scavenging, is not known. Only one possible attack on a human has been recorded, and that was way back in 1849. Yet the number of sailors consumed by Greenland sharks must be in the countless thousands. I find it difficult to imagine the terrors faced by a 19th-Century whaling crew whose vessel became trapped, then crushed in the ice (a common occurrence). The ship's timbers would have creaked and screamed as the vessel was mauled by the moving bergs. It's probably a good thing that the habits of the Greenland shark weren't known at the time, for although the men would have quickly frozen to death in the Arctic waters, the thought of what awaited their bodies in the deep would only have added to the doomed mariners' terror.

The most horrific of all documented attacks by the Greenland shark occur in seal colonies off the northeast coast of the USA and Canada. There the seals haul out into the shallows of beaches on remote islands to sleep, where the sharks creep up on them. With immense power, a Greenland shark grasps the sleeping seal and skins it alive, the skin coming off in a distinctive corkscrew pattern. Nobody is sure how or why this happens, but it may be that the seal, struggling violently to free its body from the jaws of the shark, effectively skins itself. The bloody, terrified and naked seal leaves its pelt in the shark's maw, and is then slowly tracked down and consumed alive. Death by Greenland shark must surely be one of the most gruesome ends any species on Earth can ever meet.

The Greenland shark has a slow metabolism, which makes it unlikely that it is a good model for the fast-growing megalodon. But the idea that the megalodon, like the Greenland shark, might ambush sleeping marine mammals, may have some merit. After all, the ocean is opaque, and it must have taken time for whales to evolve the acute echolocation that allows them to detect the presence of a predator nearby. There is so much that we don't know yet about the megalodon that it's wise not to discard any theories until they have been proven wrong.

Scavenging is a well-known feeding strategy for large sharks, and one which the megalodon likely used. Tiger sharks are notorious scavengers. During the age of sail they often followed ships for weeks or even months at a time. As well as feeding on any refuse tossed overboard, they were known to take advantage of burials at sea. On one occasion, a few days after the crew of a Dutch East Indiaman had respectfully consigned a colleague to the deep, they went shark fishing. Food was short, and they were delighted when they hooked a large one. But when they gutted it, they discovered the body of their dead colleague, still in his canvas shroud, in the shark's stomach. As hungry as they were, they threw the dead shark overboard.

Strangely enough, evidence suggests that sharks scavenge on human remains more frequently than they attack living people. In some cases, the identity of the scavenging shark can be made known by the marks left by its teeth on the bones of the dead human. As with the seals attacked by Greenland sharks, both tiger and bull sharks also leave a distinctive spiral pattern, known as candy caning, on bodies they attack. In this case, the pattern is formed when a shark strips the flesh from the bone.

One of the most common forms of scavenging by large sharks involves their feasting on the carcasses of whales. Whale blubber is a rich food source, just 30 kilograms being sufficient to support a 4.5-metre-long great white shark for six weeks. And because whale carcasses can weigh many tonnes, they can attract and feed large numbers of sharks. As we shall soon see, fossils show that megalodons fed on whales, though how important whale carcasses were in their diet remains contentious. Astonishingly, some sharks can subsist on plants. The bonnethead shark (*Sphyrna tiburo*), a close relative of the hammerhead shark, has an omnivorous diet of shellfish and seagrass, with seagrass comprising up to 60 per cent of its total food intake. Studies of isotopes reveal that this is almost certainly one food source not utilised by the megalodon.

Studies show that the average size of the megalodon was fairly stable throughout its 20-million-year history. But one study indicates that its body size varied with water temperature, the largest individuals being found in the coolest waters. This may relate to food availability (cold waters can be very productive), or to Bergmann's Rule, which states that the largest individuals of a species will be found closer to the poles. Bergmann's Rule arises in part from an animal's need to conserve warmth: larger bodies lose heat more slowly than smaller ones. Their great size and consequent slow loss of body warmth may have allowed the largest individual megalodons to travel far towards the poles as they fed. This is certainly the case for sperm whales today, where huge males can be found much further poleward than females and smaller males.

Some of the largest teeth of the megalodon ever found have come from rocks on the Pacific coast of South America (including Peru's Pisco Formation). It's possible that the nutrient-rich waters of the ancestral Humboldt Current gave the giant predators an extra growth boost, allowing them to reach maximal size there. The largest megalodons that swam in those seas may have reached an astonishing 100 tonnes in weight. Compare that with *Tyrannosaurus rex*, which is estimated to have weighed seven tonnes at most.

Comparing fossilised teeth of the megalodon with those of selected living shark species, some scientists estimate that a 16-metre-long megalodon would have had a head more than 4.5 metres long, with a dorsal fin the height of an average woman (1.6 metres). Its cavernous maw could swallow you and several friends at a bite. Many of the two-dimensional representations of the megalodon that you'll see in books are based solely on teeth. Several assumptions are made by the scientists who create such reconstructions, not all of which will stand the test of time. For example, as explained earlier, most use the great white shark as a model for the appearance of the megalodon, but the great white is not closely related to the megalodon, so there is little reason to assume a closely similar body form, though admittedly, many marine predators—from sharks to dolphins—are variations on the same sleek, torpedo body shape. Indeed, there are hints that the megalodon might not have looked like a scaled-up great white shark: for example, some researchers think that it may have had a shorter nose, a flatter jaw, and longer pectoral fins relative to the great white. Given our current state of knowledge, many notions can be

neither supported or refuted, making the details of reconstructions simple speculation.

A careful examination of the fossil record is slowly
yielding clues about the diet of the megalodon, much of
it in the form of tooth-scarred fragments of bone. These
humble fossils are not as likely to be picked up by collectors
as the teeth of the megalodon itself, and much evidence
doubtless continues to slip through our hands as quarries expand and erosion cuts into sediments, momentarily
freeing, then destroying, fossils. The marks left on bones
by the teeth of the megalodon are highly distinctive. The
shark bites deep, leaving gouges in the bone which bear
the impressions of the fine, even serrations characteristic of
its teeth. Occasionally a fragment of a tooth is even found
embedded in the bone or lying nearby. Among the most
common of such finds are the flipper and tail bones of
medium-sized whales and other cetaceans. This has led
some researchers to suggest that cetaceans were the megalodon's preferred prey, and even to infer a typical method of
attack. The idea is that megalodons attacked whales by severing their tail flukes and flippers, leaving them helpless so
that the shark could dismember them without risk. Great
white sharks attack some prey, such as enormous adult male
northern elephant seals by first disabling their rear flippers,
so the idea that the megalodon acted in a similar manner
is plausible.

Evidence of possible scavenging behaviour by the megalodon (or less likely another large shark) is provided by bite marks on a 27-centimetre-long flipper bone of a now-extinct baleen whale discovered in Maryland USA. The shapes of the tooth marks, known as bite-and-shake marks, indicate the shark had thrashed its head from side to side as it ripped off a chunk from the floating whale carcass—or possibly the living whale. We know the shark took at least three bites in this feeding frenzy. The fossil flipper bone, incidentally, was found by a local fossil collector, who, instead of selling it on the side of a highway, recognised its importance and donated it to the local museum. Unfortunately, so far scientists have been unable to narrow down the list of potential large shark culprits, as it has not been possible to determine whether the marks were made by a serrated tooth.

Also unearthed in Maryland was the middle portion of a fossilised whale vertebra which had a partly healed compression fracture indicating a sudden and violent trauma, possibly inflicted by a megalodon. The lower portion of the vertebra had been completely broken and then partially fused by regrowing bone, indicating the whale lived for about six weeks following the attack. At about six metres long, the unfortunate whale was mature but not particularly old. This fossilised whale bone with its evidence of healing allows us to be certain that it resulted from a failed predation attempt.

A fossilised lumbar (lower back) vertebra of a whale was discovered off the Caribbean coast of Venezuela with a broken megalodon tooth still embedded in it. The fossil is Pliocene in age—a time when the populations of the megalodon were waning, and when its teeth are rare in Caribbean sediments. The scientists who reported on the fossil suspect that the whale lost its life during the attack, and that following death its carcass floated for a while, before sinking and settling on the bottom of the ocean. But because the tooth was embedded in the vertebrae close to the time of death, it's difficult to ascertain whether the injuries were sustained by a living whale or are the result of scavenging.

A Pliocene fossilised rib bone belonging to a small, extinct kind of baleen whale, likely to be an ancestor of the humpback or blue whale, shows bite marks attributed to the megalodon. It also shows evidence of healing following the attack. Fortunately the fossil was rescued from a pile of waste material in a phosphate mine in North Carolina, before it was ground up into fertiliser or used as road material. The rib exhibits several tooth marks about six centimetres apart, and from the arc of these indentations we know the shark was fairly small for a megalodon—between four and eight metres long. The rib fragment is covered by a special kind of bone called woven bone which forms after an infection subsides. The fact that the woven bone had not been replaced by another kind of bone (compact bone) indicates that the whale probably died several weeks after the attack, before compact bone could be laid down. It's likely that the attack was made by a juvenile megalodon that struck the whale on its side, just behind the pectoral fin. The shark may have left with a chunk of flesh, but nothing more.

Some prey of the megalodon has been identified down to species level. On the southern coast of Peru, in the Pisco Formation, seven-million-year-old fragments of bones belonging to the small baleen whale *Piscobalaena nana* bear megalodon scars. Some of the tooth marks left on the skull bones are more than five centimetres long, perhaps the result of an attack by an adult megalodon. As *Piscobalaena nana* was less than five metres in length, it would have provided little more than a snack for an adult megalodon.

Not even ancient sperm whales were beyond the reach of the megalodon. A fossil sperm whale tooth bearing gouges made by a megalodon was discovered in a mine in Aurora, North Carolina. The whale tooth, which is 11 centimetres long and around five million years old, has three gouges stemming from repeated bites from large, serrated teeth. Perhaps the sperm whale turned to face its aggressor in a bid to avoid a fatal wound, but died in the fight.

There is some fossil evidence suggesting that the megalodon may have engaged in cannibalism, as a fossil megalodon tooth bearing bite marks left by another tooth of a megalodon has been found. It's possible, however, that the marks were left by other teeth in the mouth when the damaged tooth was shed, perhaps during a bout of feeding. Cannibalism in adult sharks living today, however, is fairly common, even among the fearsome great whites. They have been photographed and filmed while engaged in mortal combat, the loser becoming a meal for the victor.

We also have direct evidence of shark cannibalism in the fossil record in 300-million-year-old fossilised faeces (known as a coprolite). This particular poo fossil was discovered in a disused Canadian coal mine, and it contained juvenile shark teeth of the same species as the individual that left the faeces. One might imagine determining the species that produced a fossil poo to be plagued with difficulty, not so in the case of *Orthacanthus*, an eel-shaped shark that grew to around three metres long. It had a spiral rectum that created distinctive and easily identifiable spiral-shaped faeces.

There is also circumstantial evidence of shark-on-shark predation dating to the time when the megalodons ruled the seas. Several fossilised shark vertebrae found at the Calvert Cliff, Maryland, and dating from 23–2 million years ago, show deep gouging marks from forceful shark bites. The marks were left when one requiem shark (*Carcharhinus*) attacked another and left a four-centimetre-long tooth embedded in a vertebra, which showed signs of healing in response to the injury. This unique find not only allowed scientists to identify the predator and so confirm cannibalism, but also to establish that the attack was made on a living animal, rather than resulting from scavenging. Such informative finds are exceedingly rare, but the very fact of this fossil's existence holds out hope that direct evidence of shark-on-shark predation involving the megalodon may one day be found.

The great white, which, although a comparative pygmy, has behaviours that provide insights into the strategies that massive marine predators use to survive, and so can help inform us about the megalodon's survival traits. Great white sharks can weigh as much as 2.25 tonnes and exceed six metres in length. They are slow breeders, with females giving birth for the first time at about 33 years of age, and pregnancy lasting eleven months. Females are larger than males, and it's estimated that both sexes live for up to 70 years. Great whites maintain a body temperature that is higher than that of the water they often swim in, and keeping a body warm in cold water takes a lot of energy. Great whites can also travel enormous distances in search of food. One individual was recorded swimming from South Africa to Australia and back in nine months—a 20,000-kilometre journey.

When they reach about four metres in length, great whites begin to feed mostly on marine mammals, particularly seals. But stable isotope analysis of the vertebrae of great white sharks reveals that their diet preferences can be quite individualised, with some taking squid or other small prey in addition to seals. The very largest great whites seem to have lost the physical flexibility required to catch seals, and they feed by preference on whale carcasses. One six-metre-long specimen caught off South Australia in the 1970s revealed an unusual dietary specialisation. It was brought to the South Australian Museum in 2001 to stabilise its preservation, and the taxidermist who treated it discovered a number of large stingray spines in its head. Stingray spines break off easily, and once embedded in their victim they continue to work their way ever deeper into the flesh. One spine, which had entered through the roof of the shark's mouth, had travelled almost clean through its head, narrowly missing its brain. Why, I wondered, would a shark specialise in such potentially lethal prey?

In the 1960s and 70s, when that particular shark had already reached a large size, human hunting had almost exterminated the whales and seals that may have been its natural prey. I can only imagine the hunger-driven desperation of that enormous shark. To satisfy its voracious appetite it must have attacked the large and abundant stingrays of the region, and often suffered a victim's wrath. It is astonishing to me that there were only four recorded shark attacks on humans in South Australia during the 1970s. But perhaps back then, shark fishing and a lack of food had rendered large great whites as rare as hen's teeth.

CHAPTER 3

Origins:
The Evolution of Sharks

Until very recently, there was no agreement about the ancestry of the megalodon. Multiple, conflicting ideas about its family tree have resulted in the species being placed in no less than four different genera (*Carcharocles*, *Procarcharodon*, *Megaselachus* and *Otodus*). One of the more popular, and seemingly credible, ideas was that the megalodon was related to the living great white shark. The great white has the largest and most fiercely serrated teeth of any living shark species, and the megalodon has the largest and most fiercely serrated teeth of all time, which suggested a relationship to some. But there are significant differences. The teeth of the megalodon so completely dwarf those of the great white that it's like comparing a toothpick to a pick-axe. And the serrations on the teeth of great white sharks are irregular in size, indeed downright messy, unlike the precise and fine, steak-knife-like serrations of the teeth of the megalodon.

The theory went that, before it became extinct, the megalodon gave rise to the smaller, surviving great white shark. But as scientists looked in detail, the story started to unravel. The discovery of Hubbell's shark (*Carcharodon hubbelli*) in the 1990s was the last nail in the coffin for the theory. This missing link showed that the giant mackerel shark, *Carcharodon hastalis*, had almost certainly given rise to the great white. Teeth of the giant mackerel shark are among the most common vertebrate fossils found in Miocene marine sediments worldwide. I have found hundreds of them at the Beaumaris fossil locality, and some are enormous—far larger than the largest teeth of today's great white sharks. The teeth of the giant mackerel shark differ from those of Hubbell's shark only in lacking serrations, while the teeth of Hubbell's shark are almost identical to those of the great white, except for being less serrated. This has convinced most researchers that the great white arose from the giant mackerel shark, rather than from the megalodon. The development of large, serrated teeth indicates a diet of marine mammals, while smooth-edged teeth indicate a diet of fish. The great white shark evolved from the giant mackerel shark, so it seems that the lineage had switched to a diet of mammals.

Only recently has painstaking detective work revealed the true ancestry of the megalodon—and the results are surprising. But to make sense of the story we need to go back to the origins of the sharks themselves. Sharks are part of a group known as chondrichthyans, they all lack bones, and instead have skeletons made of cartilage. The group appeared about 480 million years ago—before there was complex life on land. There are three fundamental kinds of chondrichthyans—the various skates and rays and their relatives, the little-known chimaeras, and the sharks. Cartilage is softer than bone, and having a skeleton made of cartilage might seem to be primitive—a sort of halfway house between species that have no skeleton and those that have skeletons of bone. But in fact the cartilaginous skeleton of the chondrichthyans is highly specialised, and it evolved from a bony form. We know this because a 380-million-year-old fossil shark discovered in north-western Australia has remnant bone cells in its cartilage—a sure sign that the cartilage had taken over from bone. There are many ways in which cartilage is superior to bone. For a start it is lighter, and in a marine environment it allows sharks to swim faster, enhancing their ability to avoid predators and catch prey. It is also flexible and so able to capture and use some of the kinetic energy generated by the muscles, in a similar way to a pogo stick capturing and re-using the energy of a jump.

Sharks came into existence at a time when the Earth was warming, and some of its first coral reefs (which were very different from, and unrelated to, modern coral reefs) were expanding in the shallow, tropical waters. Anything that lacks bones leaves a patchy fossil record at best, and we know the earliest sharks from the merest skerricks, in the form of minute scales and a few fin spines entombed in the limestones that remain from these early reefs in what is now Mongolia, Siberia, China and North America. The fossils are 480 million years old, just 50 million years younger than the oldest chordate (the ancestor of all back-boned creatures), making sharks a very early branch on the evolutionary tree of creatures with a backbone.

The scales embedded in shark skin are known as denticles, and they look like miniature teeth. Unlike the scales of bony fish, which grow as the fish grows, denticles always stay the same size, with more being added as the creature increases in size. Denticles make the skin of sharks, rays and skates much rougher to the touch than that of most bony fish. Humans have long appreciated this: thousands of years ago shark skin was used as a kind of sandpaper to shape and smooth wooden objects. In modern times the shape and size of denticles on shark skin has been replicated in swimsuit materials used by elite athletes to reduce drag in the water. Early in the evolution of vertebrates, dermal denticles moved into the mouth. In 2017 a group of scientists found that the dermal denticles of the little skate (a modern cartilaginous fish that resembles a small stingray) are produced in the same location in the skate embryo as teeth in human embryos. They were able to track the development of these cells, proving that we retain the remnants of ancient fish armour in our mouths—in the form of teeth.

Nobody knows how many species of sharks existed 480 million years ago, and we have no idea what the earliest sharks looked like. But denticles predate the oldest fossil shark teeth by at least 50 million years, which suggests that the earliest sharks were toothless. They may have been filter feeders that sustained themselves on plankton. At the time they lived, the sea floor was spreading and fresh magma was adding nutrients to the water. Ocean levels were high, and extensive shallow seas covered the continental shelves. Atmospheric and oceanic oxygen levels were also high, allowing tiny phytoplankton and zooplankton to abound. This unusual constellation of conditions may have produced a plankton cornucopia that provided an evolutionary opportunity for the first sharks.

Filter feeding is a recurring theme in shark evolution, from the largest of living sharks, the whale shark, through to the basking shark and the deep-water megamouth. The strategy has evolved multiple times in multiple lineages, each time using a slightly different method. It seems ironic that the megalodon could have evolved from such inoffensive ancestors, but the 400 million years that separate the earliest sharks from the megalodon is a long time indeed. Four hundred million years ago our own ancestors were bony fish.

The oldest shark teeth in the fossil record date back 430 million years and are a sure sign that by then some shark species were evolving into active predators. The oldest surviving branch of the chondrichthyan family tree, the chimaeras, provides some clues as to what these ancient sharks may have looked like. Chimaeras, with their long, narrow bodies, large heads and sizable eyes, are very different in appearance from many modern sharks, but like sharks they have cartilaginous skeletons. They are often found in the deep sea, and include the oddly named ratfish, rabbitfish, spookfish and elephant sharks. While living species of chimaera are specialised in their own way (for example, they all have tooth plates for grinding their food rather than pointed teeth), they share a number of features with the early sharks.

I am fortunate enough to have swum with a very strange species of chimaera known as an elephant shark (or ghost shark), which is only found in shallow waters off southern Australia, New Zealand and southern Africa.

Each spring some swim into Port Phillip Bay to breed. I was such a keen fossil hunter that I often searched for fossils in Port Phillip Bay right through winter and early spring. At that time of year, the waters of the bay can still be a chilly 10°C and, despite my thick wetsuit, the frigid water soon became agonising, so my observations of elephant sharks, as fascinating as I found them, were usually fleeting.

Reaching a length of 1.5 metres, elephant sharks are boldly patterned in black and white, with large eyes and a sharp, venomous spine in front of their two dorsal fins. But their weirdest feature is their bizarre proboscis, with its fleshy disc at the end, which it uses to locate food on the sea floor. Male elephant sharks have a second bizarre feature—what appears to be a second mouth, located high on their foreheads. This toothy structure, which is hinged like a jaw, is not used for feeding, but to grasp and hold on to the females during mating.

After elephant sharks mate and the females lay their large, yellowish egg-capsules, each of which contains a single young, the adults leave the bay, disappearing into the deeper waters of Bass Strait. There they are occasionally caught by commercial fishers and sold to fish-and-chip shops, where along with other shark species they are marketed as that peculiarly Victorian delicacy known as 'flake'. A fisherman once gave me a freshly caught elephant shark. Its flesh was pale green, a colour which I can only guess fades as it ages, as I've never been served green flake. Being young and adventurous, I ate it. It tasted fine.

The fossil beds that I searched for fossil shark teeth also preserved the fossilised tooth plates of a gigantic relative of the elephant shark. They are striking fossils, being around eight centimetres long and composed of shiny black-and-white material that runs their length in bold stripes. I made a small collection of these tooth plates, which I later gave to the Museum of Victoria. The discovery of each fossil tooth plate among the pebbles and seaweed of the bay floor had me trying to imagine the creature they were once part of. The fossil tooth plates are so large that the extinct elephant shark that made them must have exceeded three metres in length. It would have been a spectacular sight, especially if it was as brightly patterned as its living descendants. How I would have loved to have seen it. But the species that produced these extraordinary fossils seems to have vanished around the time that the megalodon winked out, sometime after 4.5 million years ago.

It was not until around 380 million years ago that anything resembling a modern predatory shark arose. *Cladoselache* was closely related to chimaeras, but fast, streamlined and superficially shark-like. It grew to 1.8 metres in length and had the distinctive forked tail we recognise in many sharks today. Beautifully preserved body fossils of *Cladoselache*, many including traces of their last meals, have been found in the Cleveland Shale, a rock formation that crops out widely across the eastern United States. The stomach contents provide the earliest evidence of shark-on-shark predation in the fossil record. The fossils recording this are so well preserved that scientists can tell that *Cladoselache* attacked its prey from behind, swallowing it tail-first. To do that, it must have been very fast.

The geological timescale divides the period during which complex life thrived into three great eras: the Paleozoic, which extends from 541–252 million years ago, the Mesozoic from 252–66 million years ago, and the Cenozoic from 66 million years ago until today. Sharks, which are one of the longest lived of all vertebrate lineages, prospered through all three of these eras. Some of the sharks that lived during the earliest (the Paleozoic) were downright bizarre, and few more so than the famous Bearsden shark, *Akmonistion zangerli*. Discovered by fossil enthusiast Stan Wood in the 1970s beside a small creek in Bearsden (a part of Glasgow that is now a housing estate, making the fossil-bearing rocks sadly inaccessible), it is the most complete shark fossil ever discovered. The preservation is so good that details of blood vessels and muscles can even be discerned. Wood's discovery shows that you never know what you'll find if you keep your eyes open, even in the most ordinary-seeming of places.

No larger than a salmon, the Bearsden shark was a kind of chimaera that bore a bizarre bony crest on its head, along the top of which ran rows of sharp teeth. Nobody knows what this extraordinary appendage was for, but in light of the strange, toothed clasper on the head of the elephant shark, some suspect that it had a sexual function. Perhaps it was used for attracting or titillating female sharks. Whatever its use, I vote it as among the most remarkable anatomical structures ever evolved. Today the Bearsden shark takes pride of place in Glasgow's Hunterian Museum. If you want to venture your own opinion, it's well worth a visit.

It is only when those rare fossils showing soft-body preservation are unearthed that we get clues as to what the earliest sharks looked like. One such species, *Phoebodus*, was until recently known only from individual teeth (which are distinctive, with three cusps) as well as a few fin spines. There was much speculation about its size and form, but then some complete specimens, 365 million years old, were found in the Anti-Atlas Mountains of Morocco. Thanks to a low oxygen environment at the time of its death, incredible bodily detail was preserved. When scanned by CT, *Phoebodus* was revealed to have had a long eel-like body, as well as backward pointing teeth and a flattened skull— a shape never suspected from the previously discovered, more fragmentary fossils. The highly unusual body shape of *Phoebodus* is shared with the modern deep-sea frilled shark, yet these two creatures are only distantly related. Their similarities may be due to them sharing a highly specialised feeding strategy, which appears to involve swallowing their prey whole and their backward-facing teeth preventing its escape.

At the end of the Devonian Period of the Paleozoic Era (each era is divided into periods), about 375 million years ago, life on Earth was dealt a huge blow. At least 75 per cent of species vanished. Reef ecosystems collapsed as the oceans experienced warming, constant and recurring sea-level changes, and extensive episodes of anoxia. Biodiversity declined as the speciation rate (the rate of creation of new species by natural selection) slowed. Many species of fish succumbed during this biodiversity crisis, and directly following the extinction event most surviving sharks were pygmies—no more than 10 centimetres long. Soon, however, these small sharks were diversifying and increasing in size, until within a few million years they once again dominated the seas.

Sharks would go on to survive three more mass extinction events, a feat that they managed by being super tough, diverse and adaptable. Despite their apex predator status, most sharks are not picky eaters, meaning they are able to diversify their diet when a food source diminishes. Sharks are also efficient digesters, as evidenced by their gooey faeces devoid of solid matter. The ability to break down most of the food consumed is especially helpful in times of scarcity, such as during a mass-extinction event.

Some of the shark species that arose in the wake of the Devonian extinction event have given rise to the most ridiculous reconstructions. One such was the enigmatic *Helicoprion*, which lived around 270 million years ago in the Late Carboniferous Period. It was a true giant, growing to an astonishing seven and a half metres long. *Helicoprion* is a relative of the rat fish or chimaeras, but in its mouth was a whorl of teeth reminiscent of an elaborate circular saw. This continuous spiral of as many as 125 teeth was built up because rather than shed its teeth as other sharks do, this predator kept those in its lower jaw while it continued to produce more, incorporating the older teeth into a buzzsaw-shaped whorl.

For many years, the only fossils that palaeontologists had of *Helicoprion* were its tooth whorls. Some early reconstructions placed the whorl on the creature's nose with the snout bent upwards in a comical manner like a toothy elephant trunk. Others placed the whorl on the shark's back, and some even had it hanging off the tail. It was only when a fossil whorl containing tiny bits of cartilage was examined by CT scanner that its actual position on the lower jaw was uncovered. Although our understanding of how *Helicoprion* used its tooth whorl is still speculative, it is possible that it attacked soft-bodied prey like squid with a chopping motion of its buzz-saw tooth whorl.

Some ancient shark lineages have survived to the present day. The six-gilled sharks for example date back to around 200 million years. These primitive-looking creatures have a long, sinuous body with a single dorsal fin, a broad head and six gills instead of the usual five. Perhaps the most remarkable living sixgill is the elusive frilled shark. Rarely seen alive by humans, it resembles a deep-sea serpent. It uses its eel-like body to swim slowly in the dark, moving sinuously side to side like a snake. It has two large, beaming eyes on its monstrous head, and at the end of its snout is a mouth full of backwards-facing, three-pronged teeth. How on earth it hunts remains a mystery. We do know, from investigating the stomach contents of dead specimens, however, that it has a taste for squid.

The modern shark groups that dominate today's oceans did not come into existence until late in the Jurassic Period, about 200 million years ago. But it was not until the mid-Cretaceous Period, about 100 million years ago, that sharks began to act as top predators. These predatory sharks, however, continued to coexist with some unusual sharks that were adapted to other ecological niches, among the strangest of which were the hybodonts. We are fortunate to have an entire body fossil of one of the largest of the hybodonts, *Asteracanthus*. The specimen was unearthed from the 150-million-year-old Solnhofen Limestone in

Bavaria, Germany, and it reveals that the species sported a pair of horns on the top of its head, as well as a hard spine on its dorsal fin. The horns were curved and barbed and are thought to have been present only in males. These horny sharks had robust, conical teeth adapted to crushing, grinding or cutting. What they ate is not known, though hard-shelled molluscs is a reasonable guess.

Other bizarre sharks from the age of dinosaurs include the shell-crushing behemoth *Ptychodus*, a sluggish-moving bottom dweller that grew to about 10 metres long. Specialising in pulverising hard-shelled animals, it was able to prey on the enormous, reef-building clams of the day by picking them up directly from the sea floor. Its jaw alone was one metre wide, with upper and lower dental plates grinding the hardest biological materials with great force. Its body shape may have resembled that of the modern-day nurse shark, and it seems to have grown very slowly, achieving sexual maturity at an advanced age.

By the late Cretaceous, there existed a lineage of sharks that foreshadowed the ecological niche that the megalodon would occupy 50 million years later. The seven-metre-long *Cretoxyrhina* may have preyed on other large sharks like *Ptychodus*. With smooth, curved teeth so sharp they could shear through bone, *Cretoxyrhina* also hunted reptilian predators, including the great marine mosasaurs and plesiosaurs. Bite marks on the bones of these prey indicate

Cretoxyrhina had a super-strong bite force. A rare find from what is now western Kansas is the tooth-scarred vertebrae of a shovel-beaked dinosaur, known as a hadrosaur. Carried far out to sea, the bone must have fallen from a decomposing corpse that 86 million years ago drifted on the warm waters of America's Western Interior Seaway, a body of water that, during the Cretaceous, extended through the centre of what is now North America. Importantly, the specimen provides evidence of scavenging by the largest predatory shark from the age of dinosaurs.

Surprisingly, there is also evidence that *Cretoxyrhina* fed on pterosaurs. With a 4.5-metre wingspan, *Pteranodon* soared above the Mesozoic seas, likely diving into shark-infested waters to feed on bait fish or cephalopods. Due to their delicate and hollow nature, pterosaur bones with bite marks have been rarely found, which makes the discovery in 2018 of a *Pteranodon* vertebra with a *Cretoxyrhina* tooth fragment embedded in it a particularly important glimpse into Mesozoic marine ecology.

The smaller *Squalicorax*, a late Cretaceous shark that was typically about two metres in length, was a notable scavenger, perhaps taking the ecological role that the tiger shark occupies today. It fed on fish, turtles and pterosaurs, and traces made by its serrated teeth have been found on the bones of mosasaurs and plesiosaurs. It is commonly known as the crow shark due to its habit of scavenging the carcasses of these larger animals. Near-complete skeletons of *Squalicorax* have been unearthed in central Canada and the northern USA in what was once the Western Interior Seaway.

The megalodon belongs to the order Lamniformes (or mackerel sharks), of which there are 15 living species. They are astonishingly diverse, ranging from the great white shark to the aptly named megamouth (*Megachasma pelagios*), a harmless filter feeder of the deeper oceans. Many Lamniformes, including the salmon shark (*Lamna ditropis*) and mako (*Isurus oxyrinchus*), are at home in shallow coastal waters. Others, like the gigantic basking shark (*Cetorhinus maximus*) swim in the dark pressurised depths of the ocean, though they are also often observed in shallower water, gliding with their mouths wide open as they feed on zooplankton.

The elusive goblin shark (*Mitsukurina owstoni*), with its extendable jaws and protruding shovel-like snout, is a deep-water member of the Lamniformes, and is without doubt the most bizarre member of the order. Sluggish and rarely observed by humans, it is thought to hunt by sneaking up on its prey. As it glides along in the dark its elongated snout, known as a rostrum, detects the electric field generated by squid or fish swimming below it. The goblin shark's teeth are attached to the jaw by ligaments, and before its meal is aware of the threat from above, the goblin shark unhinges its jaws and thrusts its scraggly teeth almost eight centimetres beyond its snout. This manoeuvre is anything but sluggish and allows the shark to snatch even the speediest of prey.

The earliest known Lamniform shark is the inconspicuous *Palaeocarcharias stromeri*. At less than a metre in length and looking much like a carpet shark, it was a bottom dweller in the late Jurassic oceans. Superficially it has little in common with living Lamniformes, but one key feature linking it to them is its flexible jaws that could project forward to feed. This highly useful feature is seen in all lamnid sharks but is most readily observable today in the great white shark, and the goblin shark.

Just like our teeth, the teeth of sharks contain different types of dentine in the root-like base and inside the crown. Lamniformes, including *Palaeocarcharias stromeri*, are unique in lacking an orthodentine layer at any stage of tooth development. The orthodentine layer contains tubules through which nutrition for the tooth passes. The single exception to this is the basking shark, which has reverted to the ancestral dentine trait (that of containing an orthodentine layer).

It took a few tens of millions of years following the origination of *Palaeocarcharias stromeri* for the Lamniformes to diversify, but by the mid to late Cretaceous (100 to 66 million years ago) there were more species of Lamniformes

than of any other shark order, including the Carcharhini-
formes, or ground sharks. Today the situation is reversed,
and there are almost 20 times as many species of Car-
charhiniformes (which include tiger sharks, hammerheads
and many reef sharks), as there are species of Lamniformes.
Why did the Lamniformes boom, then dwindle? The
answer, according to some, is diet. Sea levels were about 170
metres higher in the Cretaceous than they are today, resulting in extensive inland seas where sharks thrived. Towards
the end of the Cretaceous, sea levels began to fall, reduc-
ing available marine habitat. This resulted in a substantial
decline in shark prey, a situation that was exacerbated with
the extinction of animals such as ammonites and marine
reptiles at the end of the Cretaceous. Species of sharks that
were less choosy in their diet (known as generalists), such as
many carcharhiniform sharks, were more likely to survive.

It is strange that the Cretaceous Period, which saw an
abundance of gigantic creatures evolve on land and in the
sea, did not give rise to anything like the megalodon. Food
in the form of gigantic marine reptiles abounded, and
warm coastal seaways occupied what today are dry continental margins. It's possible that huge carnivorous reptiles
such as *Kronosaurus queenslandicus*, which had a skull three
metres long and jaws studded with formidable teeth, simply outcompeted the sharks and occupied the niche of top

marine predator. And perhaps it was their extinction that then allowed the sharks to take that position.

The end for the gigantic marine reptiles came about 66 million years ago, when a 25-kilometre-wide bolide struck the Earth off the coast of what is now Mexico. The crater it made extended to Earth's mantle, almost 20 kilometres down, and it was 150 kilometres wide. Changes to the atmosphere and oceans caused by the impact caused a massive extinction event. In a geological instant the world saw the end of non-avian dinosaurs as well as the flying pterosaurs, the swimming plesiosaurs and the ammonites. Around a third of all shark species also died out at this time. Larger apex predators, which tend to have sharp, triangular teeth, were the hardest hit, in particular the mackerel sharks. They were probably specialist feeders on ammonites and marine reptiles, and as their prey disappeared, so did they. The smallest sharks and those that inhabited the deep sea were most likely to survive. In fact, the generalist fish-eating sharks increased in diversity following the extinction event. One fortunate Lamniform survivor was *Cretalamna appendiculata*, a direct ancestor of the megalodon.

With its torpedo shape and massive jaw muscles, *Cretalamna appendiculata* was a capable predator. The shape of its teeth indicates that it evolved to feed on a diet of bony fishes. It existed from about 113 million to 50 million years ago, making it one of the most enduring of all lamniform species. Most remarkable was its survival through the great extinction event that carried off the dinosaurs and most creatures on land or in the sea that weighed more than 35 kilograms. Perhaps its ability to traverse the oceans, living in varied marine environments and scavenging on whatever it encountered, allowed it to survive.

The discovery of a remarkable fossil in 1968 reveals that *Cretalamna appendiculata* also fed on larger prey. About 85 million years ago, not far from the shore of what is now Japan, a fully grown nine-metre-long marine reptile known as the elasmosaur (*Futabasaurus suzukii*) gasped its last breath. Elasmosaurs are a type of plesiosaur that have small heads, very long necks, and limbs like flippers. As the elasmosaur sank to the sea floor, up to seven *Cretalamna appendiculata* gorged on its corpse. The remains of the elasmosaur landed belly up and were covered by sediment within a few months, so beginning the long process of fossilisation. Despite a post-mortem by palaeontologists, the elasmosaur's cause of death remains unclear. But 87 shark teeth found close by, and many embedded in the elasmosaur's bones, testify to the fact that *Cretalamna* fed on the carcass, even if they did not kill the creature. The estimated length of the *Cretalamna* varied from 1.5 metres to 4.2 metres, indicating the presence of both young and old individuals.

Cretalamna appendiculata is the oldest of the apex predators that likely gave rise to the megalodon lineage. The earliest member of the megalodon's own genus, *Otodus*, is *Otodus obliquus*. The species appeared around 66 million years ago, in the wake of the bolide extinction event, and it probably arose from a *Cretalamna*-like species. *Otodus obliquus* is also the earliest member of the megatooth shark lineage. *Otodus obliquus* was several metres longer than modern great white sharks, and it had a very wide distribution across the world's oceans. Early megatooth species, like *Otodus obliquus*, have teeth with lateral cusplets, meaning they are forked, with two smaller cusps one on each side of the main blade. This tooth shape is adapted for catching and shredding swiftly swimming fish. *Otodus obliquus* survived until about 14 million years ago, so it coexisted with the megalodon and all of its predecessors. This suggests that its ecological niche was different from later megatooth sharks, perhaps being more dependent on fish.

These various species of *Otodus* form what scientists refer to as a chronospecies. Members of a chronospecies gradually evolve from one type to the next, over time. The earliest member of the megatooth chronospecies to develop serrated teeth is *Otodus auriculatus*, which first arose about

35 million years ago. It is markedly smaller than the megalodon, and its teeth retain the prominent side cuspules and shape characteristic of a fish eater, yet are coarsely serrated, suggesting some consumption of marine mammals. The teeth of *Otodus angustidens*, a species that existed from about 33 million to 22 million years ago, are largely similar to those of *Otodus auriculatus*, differing only in that they are on average larger, more finely serrated and broader. A partially complete fossil specimen consisting of 165 teeth and 23 vertebrae found in New Zealand is estimated to have been 9.3 metres long. Its teeth suggest that this species increasingly concentrated on a diet of marine mammals, but that it also ate some fish. About 22 million years ago, *Otodus angustidens* evolved into *Otodus chubutensis*, the megalodon's direct ancestor. The teeth of *Otodus chubutensis* are larger again in size and more broadly triangular. Some of its teeth retain the vestiges of side cuspules, but its other teeth are indistinguishable from those of small specimens from the megalodon.

Because the change from one species to another in the megatooth chronospecies lineage appears to have been gradual, it is difficult for palaeontologists to determine just when one species morphed into the next. This is especially the case for the transition of *Otodus chubutensis* to *Otodus megalodon*. What we do know is that the most long-lived of the *Otodus* chronospecies, some of which survived for more than 20 million years, had a broad geographic distribution, which suggests that they had a less specialised habitat and perhaps diet.

Why did the megalodon become so large? The benefits of gigantism are many. Giants are less likely to have predators, they are able to travel further, and they find it easier to retain body heat, therefore improving metabolism and activity. Perhaps increasing size and a high metabolism went hand in hand. Megalodons had the largest known newborns—over two metres long. To what extent newborn megalodons maintained a high body temperature is not known. But we do know that they grew rapidly, and so were able to quickly increase their metabolism and broaden their prey range. Perhaps these characteristics of large birth size and rapid growth were the keystone abilities that permitted the evolution of the gigantic super-carnivore that was *Otodus megalodon*.

The only living shark species that can maintain an elevated body temperature belong to the order Lamniformes, a group including the mako, porbeagle, salmon shark and great white. Because they maintain their muscles at a higher temperature than the surrounding ocean (making the muscles more powerful), these sharks can swim faster and longer, permitting long migrations. Temperature readings of the eyes and brains of makos average 24°C, about 5°C higher than the ambient sea water, while the

stomach of the great white shark reaches a temperature
of about 26°C—the highest temperature recorded for any
living shark. Despite its warm stomach, the great white is
not truly endothermic in the way that mammals and birds
are, for birds and mammals maintain a consistently high
core body temperature, an area that extends far beyond
the stomach. Megalodons are thought to have maintained
an even higher body temperature (35–40°C), begging the
question as to whether they were truly warm blooded. If
they were, then the megalodon was the only shark ever to
have achieved this. Just think of it: an enormous, warm-
blooded shark with a metabolism more like an orca than
any living shark species.

   Teeth are the business end of a shark, and it's important that they are effective in doing their work. It is likely
that the megalodon used its large, finely serrated teeth to
disable its prey then deliver a fatal strike on its victim. It
would then wait for the prey to bleed out and die, so as
to prevent injury to itself. There is one shark alive today
that preys fearlessly on the largest whales, and its teeth,
in the lower jaw at least, are very similar to those of the
megalodon. Yet this creature is a mere pygmy compared
with the extinct predator. The cookie-cutter shark lives in
deep waters, ascending from the depths at night to feed on
the monsters of the sea. It glows with an eerie green light,
and when fully grown it's only 50 centimetres long. When

it senses the presence of a whale, ray or fish, it sidles up to it, applies suction with its lips, then sinks its jaws into its victim's flesh. The spiky upper teeth offer grip, while the lower jaw vibrates like an electric knife as it cuts a semi-circular wound. The shark then deftly twists and detaches, removing a cookie-shaped piece of flesh from its victim. The bodies of some marine mammals are covered with hundreds of circular scars left by cookie-cutter sharks.

Cookie-cutter sharks can travel in schools, and they are effective at attacking large prey. One study revealed that virtually every spinner dolphin in Hawaiian waters bore scars from their attacks. Oceanographic equipment can also suffer. In the 1970s several US submarines were forced back to base because the neoprene boots of their sonar domes had been bitten through by cookie-cutter sharks. Swimmers have also been attacked, and the wounds inflicted can be severe. Such attacks can happen entirely unexpectedly anywhere in the tropics. Jack Tolley, a seven-year-old boy, was wading in shallow water in north Queensland when he had his shin cut almost to the bone by a cookie-cutter shark. And Michael Spalding, a long-distance swimmer, was attacked as he swam in calm waters between two Hawaiian islands. Feeling something soft bump into him, he suspected that it was a squid—until he felt a chunk of his flesh being yanked away. The wound was 10 centimetres in diameter and four centimetres deep, and it took months to heal. The cookie-cutter is the piranha of the shark world. It lets us guess how different our experience of the sea would be if the megalodon still survived. Even newborn megalodons would be a deadly menace. And the adults—just imagine seeing a 20-metre-long, 100-tonne shark cruising under your yacht.

CHAPTER 4

The Miocene:
The Megalodon's Heyday

The Miocene Epoch (an epoch is a subdivision of a geological period) extends from about 23 million years ago to 5.3 million years ago, and it encompasses almost the entire existence of the megalodon. Some megalodons survived into the subsequent Pliocene Epoch, but only by a few million years at most. The Miocene is the first epoch of the Neogene (the second part of the Tertiary Period). The Neogene, the 'new world', continues to the present. It is characterised by an increasingly modern-looking flora and fauna, a cooling climate and prodigious biodiversity. It is during the early Miocene that the first apes appear, and the first kelp forests.

Grasslands expanded extensively at the expense of the forests during the Miocene, heralding the arrival of grazers and the cat-like and dog-like predators that prey on them. In the fullness of time, grass, kelp and apes would come to dominate much of the habitable surface of the planet.

While the Miocene heralded a cooling trend, relative to the present climate, conditions were warm and sea levels were up to 20 metres higher than they are today. On land, the continents hosted a spectacular array of life. North America thronged with camels, horses, strange-looking short-legged rhinos and cat- and dog-like predators. Europe alone had fifteen species of rhinos, and elephants were beginning to spread into Asia and Europe. In Australia a vast freshwater lake, replete with dolphins and flamingos, occupied the centre of the continent, while rainforests fringed the east and south coasts.

In the oceans many unusual life forms flourished. The largest cowrie ever (it was the size of a construction worker's helmet) lived in the cool waters off southern Australia, the giant elephant shark swam the world's oceans, and a variety of large penguins thrived in temperate southern seas. The diversity of large sharks seemed to reach an all-time high, with the giant mackerel shark abounding alongside tiger sharks, giant thresher sharks, the megalodon and many other forms. Seals appeared for the first time, coral reefs were also flourishing and the modern whales were diversifying. In the Northern Hemisphere most species of baleen whales remained small (not exceeding 10 metres in length), but in the Southern Oceans larger whales were already present, although the gigantic blue and sei whales were yet to evolve.

My own appreciation of the incredible richness of the Miocene oceans comes from diving on the Beaumaris fossil site. Because it is exposed in a shallow marine environment, the comparison between the fossil fauna, which is about six million years old, and the one that exists today, is very obvious. The diversity of extinct creatures represented at the Beaumaris site was seemingly endless. Among the cetaceans alone, fossilised bones of ancestral right whales, *Livyatan*, two other sperm whale species, beaked whales and dolphins can all be found, along with those of dugongs and seals—species which today never coexist in nature. The sharks were incredibly diverse, including the megalodon, great white, giant mackerel shark, tiger shark, nurse shark, wobbegong, Port Jackson shark and sawfish. Teeth plates of several rays and the giant elephant fish can also be found in the deposit. Fish are represented by the teeth plates of porcupine and parrot fish, the jaws of a snapper-like species and the vertebrae of a gigantic species of moon fish. Several penguins were also present, as were albatross and the gigantic *Pelagornis*, a relative of the pelicans, with a five- to six-metre wingspan and a beak studded with sharp tooth-like projections. Diving in Port Phillip Bay, the only marine mammal I ever saw was a single dolphin, the only penguin, the occasional tiny blue, the smallest of all penguin species. The only surviving sharks were Port Jackson sharks and the elephant shark (a chimaera). But I would also encounter porcupine fish and parrot fish, and the occasional snapper. The overwhelming impression, however, was that all the largest, fiercest and most interesting creatures were gone—extinct and lost forever from the waters of the modern bay.

While the richness of the Miocene seas was truly breathtaking, the most striking thing about them was the presence of two super-predators (that is, predators that feed on other predators)—the megalodon and the enormous, carnivorous sperm whale known as *Livyatan*. *Livyatan* was as large as the largest living sperm whales but, unlike living species which have teeth only in the lower jaws, *Livyatan* had enormous teeth in both upper and lower jaws.

Throughout the 66 million years since the extinction of the dinosaurs, only in the Miocene were the oceans able to support two such enormous super-predators as megalodon and *Livyatan*. Defining a species as a super-predator, incidentally, is not straightforward. Baleen whales, which feed on krill, could be defined as predators because they eat other animals (tiny krill), so animals that feed on baleen whales might be classified as super-predators. But a predator that fed upon sharks, for example, is much more clearly a super-predator, because sharks feed upon fish or seals, which in turn feed on smaller prey, which in turn feed on krill-sized prey, so that the food pyramid that supports them has an extra level.

You can think of the food pyramid as being like the famous Egyptian pyramids at Giza. If you wanted to increase the height of such a pyramid by one block, you'd need to add another layer of blocks to the bottom. For example, if a pyramid has a base layer 10 by 10 blocks (100 blocks in all), the new base layer would need to be, say, 12 by 12 blocks, which is 144 blocks. Likewise, if a new level is added to the food pyramid (as appears to have been the case for the super-predators of the Miocene), a massive increase in the availability of food is required at the base of the food chain.

The idea that the megalodon was a super-predator has recently been boosted by one of the most exciting breakthroughs in palaeontology. Published in 2022, the research involves an analysis of the ratio of nitrogen-14 to nitrogen-15 in the fossilised teeth of the megalodon. High levels of nitrogen-15 relative to nitrogen-14 indicate that a species occupied a position high on the food pyramid. This particular study revealed that the ratio of nitrogen-15 relative to nitrogen-14 in the teeth of the megalodon is so astronomically high that the researchers concluded that it occupied a higher place on the food pyramid than any other marine species, living or extinct. So elevated is the ratio indeed that it could not result from the megalodon feeding solely on baleen whales (though this does not mean that megalodons did not at least occasionally feed on them, as is witnessed by bite marks preserved on the fossilised bones of baleen whales). But the new study does tell us that other, more carnivorous prey must have been more commonly taken. Just what this prey might have been is not yet known. One strong possibility, however, is other sharks. Because of their cartilaginous skeleton, little evidence of sharks predating on other sharks is preserved in the fossil record. During the Miocene, however, the oceans were filled with enormous sharks, with the giant mackerel shark (the ancestor of the great white shark) particularly abundant.

The nitrogen-15 study also suggests that the megalodon preyed on members of its own species—that it was a cannibal. If this was the case, the megalodon would not be the only marine species to feed off smaller members of its own kind. Tuna, for example, breed in areas where food, except for plankton, is limited. The newly hatched tuna larvae feed on plankton, but they grow rapidly, and soon they need fish protein, and the only fish that are present in sufficient numbers to feed them are younger tuna. This behaviour is so widespread that cannibalism may be the main factor limiting the population of some tuna species, including Atlantic bluefin tuna, during the earlier stages of the life cycle. In the case of the megalodon, it's easy to imagine truly enormous individuals feeding on smaller ones. Cannibalism might also account for the very specific breeding grounds of the megalodon. Such areas must have had enough food for the young sharks to feed on and grow, but also have been protected from older megalodons. Another important implication of the nitrogen-ratio study is that large great white sharks did not compete with megalodons for the same prey. Their nitrogen-15 concentrations are just too low by comparison, which reduces the likelihood that the evolution of the great white shark caused the extinction of the megalodon.

To understand the full implications of the findings of the nitrogen-ratio study, imagine a gigantic super-lion that fed only on other lions. It takes millions of grass plants to feed a few thousand zebras, which in turn feed just a few lions. There are around 20,000 lions in the world today, and a population of that size would be sufficient to support just a few tens to a few hundred of our hypothetical super-lions. And that's just not a large enough population to survive in the long term. We'd probably need a population of hundreds of thousands of lions to support a viable population of super-lions over the long term, which would require a much more productive, lion-friendly Earth.

Livyatan was the second super-predator of the Miocene seas. It was around the size of the largest sperm whale alive

today (17 metres long), and it is the megalodon's only serious challenger for the title 'largest predator that ever lived'.
It had a shorter snout than the living sperm whale, and
teeth in both the upper and lower jaws, perfect for keeping
steady hold of thrashing prey. The longer snout of the living
sperm whale, with teeth only in the lower jaw, is adapted
to feeding on large squid, by suction. The temporal fossa
(the depression in the sides of the skull where the muscles for mastication attach) of *Livyatan* was enormous—
twice the size of that of living sperm whales, and three
times as large as those of an orca. These massive muscles
allowed *Livyatan* to close its jaw with great force. Its teeth
are stupendous—like huge, fat bananas in shape. Yet they
are extraordinarily blunt, and must have acted like mal-
lets, inflicting severe crushing wounds on whatever they
encountered. How *Livyatan* dismembered its prey to swallow the pieces, remains enigmatic, as its teeth offered no
way to sever flesh. Perhaps it shook its victims to pieces.

Most specimens of *Livyatan* have been found in the
Pisco Formation in Peru. There, baleen whales make up
more than 80 per cent of fossils. At the time *Livyatan* was
at its peak, baleen whales were becoming larger, and they
could have provided a rich source of energy for the predator. It's tempting to imagine that they made up most of
Livyatan's prey, but we have very little real evidence, by
way of fossil bones bearing bite marks, about what *Livyatan*

ate. It could just as easily have fed on other kinds of sperm whales, of which five types coexisted with *Livyatan* during the Miocene.

The megalodon and *Livyatan* were among the very largest creatures living in the Miocene seas and, extraordinarily, both were warm-blooded. There is simply nothing like these two species in the world's oceans today nor, as far as we know, in oceans of the past. The oceans of the Miocene Epoch must have been rich beyond the wildest imaginings of the most optimistic fisher that ever wet a line. But, even so, it's very hard to conceive of an ocean so rich that it could have supported more than a few thousand adult, warm-blooded, 60-tonne hyper-carnivorous megalodons and killer sperm whales.

Nobody knows why the Miocene oceans were so productive. Where did the food come from to sustain such ravening hordes? Perhaps the kelp forests, which arose in the Miocene, provide a clue. Charles Darwin said of the kelp groves of Patagonia, 'I can only compare these great aquatic forests with the terrestrial ones in the inter-tropical regions.' Kelp requires cool waters to grow, and cool waters are productive because nutrients flow up from the bottom layers to the sunlit regions. If the upper layers get too warm, it's much more difficult for nutrient-rich lower water to circulate. Perhaps the conditions that favour kelp were more widespread in the Miocene. Whatever happened to the oceans, it resulted in a world that still has kelp, but has been stripped of its super-predators—*Livyatan* and the megalodon.

The fate of life on land during the Miocene might offer some insights into the changes that affected the oceans. Prior to the Miocene, Europe and North America supported substantial forests and many mammals were relatively small, with a limited biodiversity of large mammals. But during the Miocene, grasslands spread at the expense of forests, and enormous biodiversity and biomass sprang up. North America and Europe resembled the richest plains of East Africa today, with their countless herds of wild mammals. After the Miocene the world became colder and less productive, and the heyday passed for Europe and North America's mammal diversity. Perhaps there's a 'sweet spot' in world climatic conditions where large numbers of large animals can flourish. Too warm, and there's not enough food. Too cold, and productivity is again limited.

The megalodon was distributed widely throughout the tropical and temperate waters of the world during the Miocene. Fossilised teeth have been found in coastal sedimentary deposits of every continent except Antarctica. And judging from the fossil record, the megalodon consistently occupied the Atlantic Ocean, the Caribbean, California and Australia throughout the entire Miocene Epoch. Scientists suspect that the megalodon preferred shallow, warm seas in tropical and subtropical areas, but because fossils from deeper parts of the ocean are rarely found, it's possible that the great shark also haunted the high and deep seas as well.

During much of the Miocene, expansive seaways separated North and South America, as well as Eurasia and Africa. These seaways may have allowed the megalodon and other marine animals to undertake long migrations. Some seas, however, remained isolated, and it seems possible that distinct sub-populations of the great shark developed there. This is particularly the case for nearly enclosed seas such as the Mediterranean as it was in the later Miocene, where there is some fossil evidence suggesting that the megalodons became pygmies. Fossil teeth locations in Spain, France and elsewhere are from individuals estimated to be no more than 4.5 metres long. Did a lack of prey restrict their growth? Or did the largest sharks simply leave the area? If the Mediterranean megalodon population was isolated and of small body size, the megalodons join the dwarf elephants, hippos and other creatures of diminished size which evolved in more recent times in the Mediterranean region. Moreover, because the Mediterranean Sea dried up entirely at the end of the Miocene Epoch 5.3 million years ago, its population of megalodons must have perished.

CHAPTER 5

Extinction

As the Miocene Epoch gave way to the Pliocene, the world began to change. Temperatures dropped, and the great savannahs of Europe and North America were gradually depleted of their diversity. Many of the surviving lineages of land mammals, such as elephants, rhinos and bovids developed gigantism, perhaps a response to the cooling conditions. As the Pliocene progressed, the most wondrous diversity the Earth had ever seen in the marine realm was also lost. The reasons for these changes are still debated, and it is only by examining the fossil record in ever more detail, using both traditional methods as well as with the latest technologies that answers will be found.

The megatooth (*Otodus*) lineage had thrived for almost 60 million years before the extinction of its terminal member, the megalodon, which occurred at some point in the Pliocene Epoch (5.3–2.6 million years ago). For 50 million years successive members of the lineage had flourished and grown ever larger. And all the while the Earth itself had changed: continents moved across the oceans, the climate heated then cooled, and faunas evolved, migrated and died out. And through it all the megatooth shark lineage thrived. So why, quite suddenly, in relatively recent geological times, did the megalodon, the last of the lineage, become extinct?

Many of the key facts pertaining to its extinction remain unknown. We cannot say with any certainty when, how or why these colossal sharks vanished. Let's look at the evidence we have, how it was gathered, and what flaws exist in the various scientific methods used. The most important task is to establish the 'when' of the extinction. This is critical because unless we know when a species became extinct, it is a struggle to pinpoint the cause—whether climatic, life-cycle disruption, competition with other species, or some other factor.

We are so far from establishing the precise time of the extinction of the megalodon that we must work within an 'extinction window' spanning at least two million years—between about 4.5 and 2.6 million years ago. Such a high degree of uncertainty about the extinction time of a large vertebrate that survived until relatively recently is unusual. We know, for example, that *Tyrannosaurus rex* became extinct 66,043,000 years ago, give or take a couple of hundred thousand years. And we know that the last population of woolly mammoths, which lived on Wrangel Island, died out around 3700 years ago. This degree of precision is possible because the extinction of *T. rex* resulted from a global catastrophe—an asteroid colliding with Earth—which left a global signature that can be easily traced and dated, and the extinction of the mammoth occurred so recently that highly accurate methods such as Carbon-14 dating can be deployed.

Carbon-14 dating is just one of the methods, known as radiometric dating, that use radioactive elements to accurately date fossils. Radiometric dating relies on the principle that isotopes (forms of an element whose nuclei contain the same number of protons, but different numbers of neutrons), including those of carbon, uranium and potassium, experience radioactive decay at a constant and unique rate. By measuring the ratio of the isotope and its daughter produce (the element it decays into), the time since the material was laid down can be determined. The armoury of dating techniques deployed by scientists has recently been augmented by luminescence dating, which involves analysis of quartz crystals and other materials in the rock surrounding the fossils. It can be used to determine when the sediments were last exposed to sunlight. In an ideal case, scientists use several methods, and if they all produce the same result, the date is considered secure. Despite the availability of this battery of sophisticated technologies, various impediments limit their utility when dating the extinction of the megalodon.

Radiocarbon dating is useful only for fossils less than 50,000 years old. For older fossils scientists commonly use uranium series dating, which can be used to date stalagmites and other carbonates in caves, and corals. But these techniques are of little use when trying to estimate the extinction date for the megalodon, because most aren't suited to analysing the marine sediments megalodon fossils occur in. Marine fossils are occasionally dated using strontium isotope stratigraphy (SIS), which compares the ratio of strontium-87 to strontium-86. At any point in time Earth's oceans contain a uniform value for this ratio, but the value fluctuates over time due to geological processes. When a shark is alive, strontium is incorporated into its teeth from the surrounding seawater, which then acts as a kind of time capsule representing the value of the strontium ratio in the ocean at the time, and so allowing the fossil to be dated. Enamel from sharks' teeth has been successfully dated using SIS, including enamel from a five-million-year old fragment of a tooth from the megalodon itself, which was found inside the nucleus of a nodule formed of iron and manganese that had been dredged from the seabed 4600 metres below the surface of the Atlantic Ocean. So far, however, this method has not been deployed widely enough to be useful in helping to determine the megalodon's extinction date.

Luminescence dating can be applied to a sand grain from the sediment surrounding a fossil. While the grain is exposed to sunlight, electrons cannot accumulate. But when it is buried, electrons released by the decay of radioactive elements begin accumulating in the flaws of the quartz crystal lattice. By counting the electrons released from the quartz grain when it is exposed to light (the samples have to be kept in the dark until they are analysed), researchers can determine how long it has been buried. But the flaws in the crystal lattice of a grain of quartz typically become fully filled with electrons after around 200,000 years, which is the limit for this technology, making it of little use for dating the extinction of the megalodon, which occurred at least 2.6 million years ago.

Other conventional methods of dating fossils include examining the position of the specimen in the stratigraphic column, or trying to date the microfossils (which are abundant and left by animals that evolve quickly) in the sediments surrounding the fossil in question. This might sound like a straightforward process. After all, wind and water carry debris and biological matter, including microfossils, to the bottom of seas, lakes and swamps where they form a sedimentary pile, with the most recent on the top (at least in geological deposits that have not been distorted or over-turned). Scientists could search through the pile, find the most recent megalodon tooth, identify and date the sur-rounding microfossils, and so home in on an extinction date. But this is trickier than it appears.

In part this is because the teeth of the megalodon are among the hardest and most enduring of all fossils. They can survive being eroded out of the sediments they were originally deposited in and can become redeposited in sediment of a younger age. On some beaches and rivers in Europe and North America today, it's possible to find teeth of the megalodon buried in mud and sand alongside Coca Cola cans. If those sediments were to be deeply buried, pre-served and turned to stone, millions of years in the future palaeontologists might make the mistake of concluding that the great shark and Coca Cola coexisted.

The youngest fossil megalodon teeth reported in the scientific literature are purported to be from the Pleisto-cene Epoch (2.58 million to 11,700 years ago), and some have even been mooted to be Holocene in age (11,700 years to the present day). Among these supposedly recent specimens are several worn and broken teeth that were found by amateur collector Samuel Purple, who was the manager of Lomita Quarry in California in the 1920s. A century ago the art of dating fossils, and the methods used to extract them from the rocks were rudimentary compared with current methods. A modern palaeontologist reading the old report can find many clues suggesting that the age given is questionable. The fact that the teeth were worn and broken is one such clue. This could indicate that they might have been eroded out of their original rocky tomb and redeposited in more recent rocks, a possibility not considered at the time. To make matters worse, the teeth were probably excavated using dynamite. The quarry had been dug into rocks spanning a wide range of ages, and the teeth may have been blasted a long way from the rocks they originally occurred in, leading the person who picked them up to mistakenly associate them with more recent rocks. Such factors mean that doubts about the antiquity of Purple's megalodon teeth are now so great that the age given in the original paper is discounted by most researchers.

Some of the better-documented of the supposedly geologically young teeth of the megalodon were collected during the expedition of HMS *Challenger*, a survey ship administered by the British Admiralty and the Royal Society to make a voyage around the world, charting the oceans, between 1872 and 1876. The ship sampled the oceans over transects extending 125,000 kilometres, recording hundreds of depth observations, and dredging the sea floor. One of the more spectacular finds occurred in 1875 when *Challenger* was sampling near Tahiti at a depth of over 4000 metres. When the dredge came up, the crew found in it two 10-centimetre-long megalodon teeth. These were duly deposited in a museum drawer where they lay undisturbed until 1959, when they were examined by zoologist Vladimir Tschernezky. The enterprising Tschernezky had a particular interest in cryptozoology, the study of animals that are imagined to exist but whose existence is yet to be proven. Some previously cryptid animals have indeed turned out to be alive in the modern day, including the mythical kraken (the colossal squid) and the majestic gorilla. But others, such as the yeti and the Loch Ness monster, remain in the fantastical sphere.

Tschernezky came to the conclusion that one of the dredged-up megalodon teeth was a mere 11,700 years old, and that the other was about 24,000 years old. He had calculated both dates by examining the growth rates of the manganese dioxide concretions, or nodules, which had developed on the surface of the teeth. At best, however, such concretions merely give an indication of the time since the teeth were exposed last to seawater—they may have had a long history contained in the rock prior to that. Today, it is considered likely the fossil teeth were eroded from older sediments close to the coastline and were carried into the deep, or that they had experienced multiple cycles of burial and exhumation, and are far older than Tschernezky estimated. We also know, as a result of more recent studies, that the growth rate of manganese dioxide nodules is not constant over time, as Tschernezky had imagined, but varies depending on local conditions. To add to the confusion, Tschernezky had estimated a nodule growth rate almost thirty times greater than the rate established by later studies.

The most recent fossils of the megalodon that appear to have lain undisturbed since they fell to the sea floor, and where the surrounding sediments can be reliably dated, hail from the Pliocene (5.3–2.6 million years ago). Such fossils have been found across the world. But even if we are able to accurately date most of these fossils, the extinction date of the megalodon would remain inconclusive. This is because an absence of fossils in the fossil record does not necessarily mean that a creature has become extinct.

One of the most famous dictums in palaeontology was formulated in 1982 by researchers Philip Signor and Jere Lipps. It states that 'since the fossil record of organisms is never complete, neither the first nor the last organism in a given taxon will be recorded as a fossil'. This idea has been tested and found to be true. For example, the most recent fossils of the coelacanth date back 66 million years, and it was long assumed that coelacanths had become extinct with the dinosaurs—until a living one turned up off the coast of Africa in 1938. The absence of fossils might be a consequence of many factors, including a lack of samples from relevant deposits, preservation bias (fossils only being preserved in certain conditions not reflected in the known fossil record), or the misidentification of specimens.

The dilemma posed by the Signor-Lipps dictum has led scientists to turn to computer modelling, based on probabilities, in the hope of obtaining more accurate estimates of the time of extinction of many species, including the megalodon. But even when using such methods, problems are frequently encountered. Computer models are only as reliable as the information that is fed into them. A pioneering effort at using computers to estimate the extinction time of the megalodon was made in 2014, when a research team applied a modelling method known as Optical Linear Estimation (OLE) to the problem. Their results caused something of a stir among palaeontologists, for they suggested that, on the balance of probabilities, the great shark had most likely become extinct as recently as 2.6 million years ago, though they also thought it possible, but less likely, that the extinction had occurred as early as 3.5 million years ago. The OLE method derives the most likely time of extinction from the distribution of dates attributed to the most recent fossils. The 2014 study drew on the publicly accessible paleobiology database (from museums across the world) for its samples. This database includes some dubiously identified specimens (possibly not the teeth of the megalodon at all), as well as specimens whose precise place of collection (and thus age) is uncertain. When these deficiencies were revealed, many scientists became sceptical of the extinction dates given in the paper.

A more recent piece of research, from 2019, which also used OLE, but relied only on the most reliably dated fossils, gave an earlier likely extinction date of around 3.6 million years, but with a possible, less likely extinction date of 4.1 million years. Yet even this study has not ended the controversy, for the sample of well-dated and securely identified teeth it used comes from a highly restricted geographic area in western North America (sediments in California and Baja California in Mexico). In presenting their findings, the researchers noted that their extinction date was broadly similar to that of the last recorded dates of the species from sediments in Japan, the north Atlantic and the Mediterranean (presumably from sharks that invaded the Mediterranean after its waters flooded back in the early Pliocene), but that no detailed study had been carried out on the fossils of these regions. California and Baja California encompass just a tiny fraction of the megalodon's distribution, and we cannot assume that the great shark did not survive outside this restricted region after 3.6 million years ago.

Research on the distribution of the megalodon shows that it was truly cosmopolitan, occurring in all tropical and temperate seas. There are some indications that it reached its maximum distribution in the Late Miocene (between 11 million and about five million years ago), and a statistical analysis of the fossil record suggests that after five million years ago it experienced a decline in numbers as well as in its geographic range. It is possible that the decline in both abundance and distribution are related. If there was a decline in abundance after five million years ago, this may mark the beginnings of the bleak road to extinction for the megalodon. Having looked carefully at this study, however, I'm unconvinced that either decline is real. The megalodon may have remained abundant and widespread right up to the end, its apparent decline in the Pliocene resulting from a lack of appropriate sediments and fossils. At present we must admit that we just don't know, for there are just too few securely dated fossils from too few sites globally from the critical time-period to produce a convincing conclusion.

While we can't answer the 'when' of the megalodon's extinction, we must at least try to address the 'why'. And to do this we need to think about what kind of world the great shark was living in when it met its end. Over the past 50 million years Earth's climate has gradually cooled (albeit with intermittent, smaller, substantial phases of warming), largely due to the movement of its tectonic plates. The continental masses are constantly, yet slowly, changing configuration and as they do the distribution of ocean currents is altered and new mountain chains are formed, both of which influence the flow of cold air from the poles to the equator. As continents converge towards the poles, the presence of snow and ice increases, and these factors, along with the Milankovich cycles (the changing eccentricity of Earth's orbit, the angle of Earth's tilt and the wobble of Earth's axis), meant that about 2.5 million years ago the Earth experienced persistent oceanic cooling, along with Northern Hemisphere glaciations and the development of permanent ice sheets. Although the extent of these ice sheets ebbed and flowed with the cycle caused by Earth's axial tilt, on the whole ice increased, and the global sea level dropped.

This change in climate had the potential to directly impact the megalodon by reshaping its distribution. Some research suggests that the species was dependent on warm waters of between about 12°C and 27°C. Yet this idea is at odds with the scientific data indicating that the great shark was endothermic, maintaining a higher body temperature than even the great white shark, which can roam into waters as cool as 12°C. If a cooling climate was indeed directly responsible for the extinction, it raises an important question: did the extinction happen at the same time everywhere, or did the megalodon become extinct in various geographic regions at different times?

There are many ways that a change in temperature could have directly or indirectly affected the megalodon. Perhaps the cooling restricted available habitat so much that a viable population could not survive. Alternatively, the megalodon's prey might have adapted to the cooler temperatures and migrated into frigid waters that the shark could not enter. The great whales at least seem to have followed this trajectory, spending the summer feeding in subantarctic waters. But just how dependent the megalodon was on whales for food remains a question.

Another possibility involves a disruption to its nursery grounds. To date five nursery grounds have been documented—in the Tarragona Basin, Spain, at Calvert Cliffs, Maryland, in Bone Valley, Florida, and in the Gatún and Chucunaque Formations, Panama. But of these, only parts of the Bone Valley Formation in Florida dates to 5.3–3.6 million years ago—the period when the megalodon likely become extinct. It seems possible that suitable nursery grounds for the megalodon were highly restricted, and that by the time of its extinction, all megalodon births took place at this single location.

The Bone Valley Formation was deposited in warm, shallow water in what is now Florida, and because the sea level fell as much as 125 metres by the height of each glacial cycle, this shallow water habitat may have disappeared at such times. The loss of nursery grounds would be a viable hypothesis if the megalodon had indeed survived until 2.6 million years ago, when the ice ages started. But because the latest research points to about 3.6 million years ago as the most likely extinction date of the great shark, it may not have been a factor.

Another possibility is the loss of the megalodon's migration routes. It is difficult to imagine that megalodons found all the resources they required to complete their life cycle in just one region of the ocean, making it highly likely that they followed globe-straddling migration routes as they moved from nursery grounds to feeding grounds and back. Until it closed about 2.8 million years ago, the Central American Seaway separated North from South America. If there was only one global population of the great shark, which birthed in the Bone Valley area of Florida, and used the Central American Seaway to access feeding grounds in the Pacific, the closure of the seaway as sea levels dropped could have been fatal. It's possible also that the seaway became too shallow for megalodons to use some time before its complete closure, perhaps as early as 3.6 million years ago. Was this how the great shark's tenure on Earth ended? Testing this idea will not be easy. It would involve a global study, using highly precise dating methods, of all the deposits that mark the important life stages of the megalodon.

Whatever the case, it's clear that the closure of the Central American Seaway had grave consequences for the global marine ecosystem. Its drying up put an end to the east–west currents that brought nutrients from the Pacific into the Atlantic, as well as terminating the dispersal of marine organisms from the tropical Pacific into the tropical Atlantic. It's possible that the closure of the Central American Seaway diminished ocean productivity overall, and thus impacted on the availability of the megalodon's prey.

Alternatively, global cooling may have somehow triggered a drop in biological productivity that left the food pyramid too narrow to support the megalodon. Whatever happened to the world's oceans between three and five million years ago, we know that it had a massive impact on biodiversity. It is thought that by the Late Pliocene (2.6 million years ago) a third of all large marine animals had become extinct, including numerous odd-looking creatures that have no analogue in the current oceans. Gone were the dwarf baleen whales (*Piscobalaena nana*) that some populations of megalodons at least occasionally preyed on. Gone too were the bizarre toothless walruses (*Valenictus*) of the eastern Pacific Ocean, the tropical belugas (*Bohaskaia monodontoides*), and the fantastical walrus-faced whales (*Odobenocetops*) which had two backwards-pointing tusks, one of which was often much longer than the other. The only known aquatic sloth *Thalassocnus* also disappeared at around this time. This strange creature had especially dense bones, similar to those of the earliest whales, which helped reduce buoyancy. Unlike its modern tree-dwelling cousins, it swam in the ocean shallows, feeding on marine plants such as kelp, and propelling itself along with elongated, paddle-like hands and feet. All of these very different creatures thrived in abundance in the eastern Pacific Ocean, along the west coast of South America, where the Humboldt Current flows today. Their demise brought to an end one of the most distinctive ocean biomes ever to exist.

The fossil record of the oceans of the Northern and Southern Hemispheres tell somewhat different stories of whale evolution, and this has implications for the extinction of the megalodon. In the Northern Hemisphere, smaller whales that lived in warm shallow waters dominated until towards the end of the Pliocene, when they were replaced by larger whales that inhabited the open ocean and were capable of enduring icy cold waters and of undertaking extensive migrations to exploit the increased seasonal productivity at the poles. In the Southern Hemisphere, however, larger whales (up to 10 metres long) are known from the late Miocene onwards, and they overlap with the megalodon at a number of fossil locations in Australia and elsewhere. At the locality in western Victoria where I found my first fossilised tooth of the megalodon, there is even evidence of megalodons feeding on such whales. So if, as is often asserted, the great shark became extinct because of the demise of the smaller cetaceans in the Northern Hemisphere, why did it not survive in the south, where it was already adapted to feeding off the great whales that would inherit the oceans? Interestingly, following the extinction of the megalodon, the larger baleen whales continued to flourish, eventually giving rise to the giant blue and sei whales of today.

A very different possible cause of extinction involves an increase in predatory competition. Major changes were taking place in the composition of marine predators during the Pliocene. The modern-day great white shark, *Carcharodon carcharias*, as well as the killer whale, *Orcinus orca*, were experiencing evolutionary surges. However, in the case of the orca, its presence in the Pliocene is evidenced by a mere two fossils. Could competition from these apex predators have driven the megalodon to extinction?

This could have happened through competition for food. We know that some groups of killer whales hunt marine mammals, and they are occasionally observed hunting adult humpback whales and calves, large beaked whales and even blue whales. In 2021 an incredible event was witnessed from a whale-watching boat off the coast of Western Australia. About sixty killer whales hunting in a pack took down a juvenile blue whale or adult pygmy blue whale, taking turns at harassing the poor beast until it succumbed to exhaustion. It is possible orcas and megalodons could have been competing for some of the same prey. But the data remains so thin that it's hard to make the case that orcas drove the megalodon to extinction through competition for food. Alternatively, orcas are known to hunt and kill great white sharks, so it's possible, though unlikely in my view, that direct predation by orcas on megalodons could have had an impact.

Could the rise of the great white shark have had a deleterious impact on the megalodon? We first see the ancestral species *Carcharodon hubbelli*, in the late Miocene, when it was restricted to the Pacific Ocean. But by four to five million years ago it had evolved into the great white shark *Carcharodon carcharias* and had expanded its range to become truly global. Several Pliocene fossil deposits contain evidence of the coexistence of *Carcharodon hubbelli* or *Carcharodon carcharias* and the megalodon. One such deposit is the Grange Burn locality in western Victoria, which dates to about five million years ago. The great white shark was a pipsqueak compared to the megalodon, and studies of nitrogen isotopes suggest that they had different diets. This finding is not, however, entirely conclusive. A recent study of the isotopes of zinc in the enamel of fossil teeth of the megalodon and the great white shark indicate that at around the time of the megalodon's extinction, the two species fed off the same kind of prey. Curiously, the higher up the food chain you are, the lower the zinc isotope ratios in your teeth. But just because the two species fed on the same prey does not prove that competition for food caused the extinction of the megalodon. The use of zinc isotope ratios, however, does open a new and potentially fruitful pathway for studying extinct species. Regardless of whether or not adults of both species preyed on the same species, there may have been sufficient overlap of ecological niche at some point in the life cycle to have an impact on the megalodon. For example, it's possible that fully grown great white sharks were in direct competition for prey with juvenile megalodons. Or indeed that great whites could successfully prey on juvenile megalodons.

It seems to me that two factors are likely to have contributed to the extinction of the megladon. The most important is the reduction in oceanic productivity, as witnessed by the many extinctions that occurred, during the Pliocene. Perhaps the high position on the food pyramid occupied by the megalodon really was its Achilles heel. If so, that vulnerability may have been exacerbated by a curious feature of some sharks—that females tend to be larger than males. In mammals like sperm whales, females are about a third the size of males, meaning that there can be about three times as many of them for a given amount of food. This gives the population a buffer in times of adversity. But in the great white shark, females are considerably larger than males. Limits on food availability in the current oceans mean that only a few thousand adult female great white sharks may exist at any one time. This is such a small population that it leaves them vulnerable to various shocks, including a temporary decrease in food availability and an increase in predation. Given their enormous size and high body temperature (which requires a lot of food to maintain) perhaps there were very few adult female megalodons in existence at any one time. If so, the species may have always lived on a knife edge, vulnerable to any decline in oceanic productivity.

The passing of the megalodon must have had a profound impact on ocean ecosystems; in all ecosystems, the removal of the largest predator has consequences for the lesser predators and their prey. We can gain some insights about what might have happened from modern examples of changes in predator numbers in the oceans. In the Gansbaai area off the western cape of South Africa, a pair of killer whales has recently begun to specialise in preying on great white sharks. They somehow hunt the sharks down, then eat their liver, and sometimes their heart. Great white sharks have begun to avoid the area where the orcas hunt, which has allowed bronze whaler sharks, which are preyed on by great whites, to increase in abundance, and now the bronze whalers are being attacked by the orcas as well. As a consequence of the decline in great white sharks in the area, the numbers of cape fur seals is also increasing, and because the seals eat the critically endangered African penguin, and compete with them for small pelagic fish, the penguin is declining.

The fossil record has yet to be examined for evidence of the impacts that the extinctions of the megalodon and *Livyatan* might have had on the ecosystems of the oceans. We are, I think, only at the beginning of our journey of understanding that greatest and most mysterious predator, the megalodon, and how its extinction helped shape the modern world.

CHAPTER 6

Charms, Tools and Jewels

Extinction is forever, but the extinction of the megalodon was not the end of its story, at least as far as humans are concerned. Rather it laid the foundation for a new story, in which the fossils it left behind have exerted a powerful influence on the human imagination. Knowledge that megalodon teeth are the fossilised remains of a great predator has spawned a new monster in the human imagination, one that has grown with each technological advance in our ability to visualise and portray the beast. And fossil shark teeth have played a key role in the development of the earth sciences, as well as sparking the development of novel scientific technologies and methods of analysis.

Scientists estimate that there were 272 teeth in the mouth of the megalodon. The teeth were arranged in rows and stacks of four, one atop another at various stages of development, with replacement teeth coming up behind the one in use. The teeth all start out as hollow enamel crowns, which are filled with pulp as they grow, until finally a root forms. If you find hollow enamel crowns in a fossil deposit, you've found the place where a shark died, rather than one where it shed a worn-out tooth.

In the reconstructed jaws of the megalodon the 272 teeth are divided into four quadrants (right and left upper jaws, and right and left lowers). That's 68 teeth per quadrant, stacked in fours in rows of 17. As in all sharks, the convex face, which many see as the 'front' of the tooth, is in fact the rear-facing surface. Although the shape of the teeth varies from row to row, it's not always possible to assign a tooth to a particular row. The lower teeth of the megalodon tend to be more symmetrical—and they narrow from the base sooner than the uppers, which tend to curve more posteriorly. The teeth can also change in shape as the shark ages.

The smallest teeth are at the rear of the jaw, the rear-most sometimes being little more than stubs. In the upper jaw, the teeth do not simply increase in size towards the front of the mouth, for the tooth third from the front is somewhat small relative to those on each side of it. The very largest teeth are the first and second from the front in the upper jaw. They can be massively broad as well as long and can weigh as much as 1.4 kilograms each.

Fossil shark teeth with deformities are sometimes found, and some collectors will pay extra for a distorted tooth. Some of these deformities are the result of injury. Teeth with a double or split crown, for example, can result from injury to the tooth germ layer—the tissue that generates each tooth in the tooth stack. Teeth with split or double crowns are sometimes found in great white sharks that feed on stingrays, the damage being caused when a stingray spine penetrates the shark's jaw and injures the tooth germ. Every tooth that is budded from the damaged tooth germ will then carry evidence of the injury. Other deformed megalodon teeth resemble cockscombs or have twisted crowns. The causes of these deformities are not known, though possibilities range from genetic defects to infections. Such specimens have great potential scientific value and merit further study as they may reveal hitherto unknown aspects of the life of the megalodon.

Fossil shark teeth are composed of three parts, each of which can differ in colour in ways that enhance their beauty. The root is a thickened bony mass which lacks enamel and which, in life, was embedded in the gum. In the centre of the root is a small hole, though which nerves and blood vessels passed, nourishing the living tooth. The bourlette is a band of very thin enamel that lies above the root on the convex, inward face of the tooth. Above that is the enamel-covered crown, which was the cutting part of the tooth.

Sharks' teeth are, along with ammonites and trilobites, among the most sought after of all fossils. And they are some of the most abundant of Earth's vertebrate fossils. At some localities, despite decades of collecting, fossilised teeth of large species like the megalodon are still regularly found. This abundance comes about because many shark species completely replace their dentitions every few weeks, resulting in the generation of huge numbers of teeth over a shark's lifetime. This is especially true for long-lived species like the megalodon, which was capable of producing tens of thousands of teeth over its century-long life. Multiplied by all the individuals of the species that have ever lived over the 20-million-year span of the megalodon's existence, countless millions of teeth must have fallen to the bottom of the ocean and nestled into sediments. And because shark teeth are among the hardest and most enduring of all organic materials, their chance of becoming fossilised is greater than most.

The process of fossilisation alters a shark's tooth in many ways. One curious feature of many large fossil shark teeth is that their roots bear deep, horizontal cracks. These seem to result from expansion of the root and dentine layer as a result of osmosis, a process that may have begun soon after the tooth was ejected from the shark's mouth and before it was buried deep in sediment. The discarded teeth of sharks are also sometimes damaged by marine organisms, some of which are powerful enough to drill holes into shark's teeth. The holes these organisms leave are distinctive, with smooth, almost polished sides. It's unclear which kind of organism makes the perforations, but marine bivalves and worms are known to drill similar holes in calcareous rocks, which they use for shelter.

Once buried, shark teeth are affected by a process called permineralisation. Minerals dissolved in water, such as silica, calcium and iron, percolate down through the sediments and accumulate in the porous organic structure of the teeth. These minerals eventually give rise to the striking colouration on the enamel, bourlette and root of many fossil shark teeth. This process can happen rapidly or over millions of years. Some deposits lack dissolved minerals, and they yield white fossil teeth. When a fossil shark tooth is unearthed, the next stage of the journey begins, the destinations of which are as varied as fate itself. Sometimes even the most durable fossil teeth are ground to dust by the restless energy of the sea or the powerful current of a river. Sometimes all that remains is a rounded nubbin of dentine, while at other times a near perfect tooth is simply reburied in sediment.

If a fossil tooth falls into human hands, it can become many things, from a humble tool to a magic charm, or a precious jewel. Human interactions with fossils of the megalodon go back further in time than museums have existed, further back indeed than our knowledge that the teeth are relics of a giant, extinct predator. The association may even predate the dawn of our own species, *Homo sapiens*. Upright apes began making stone tools 3.3 million years ago, and megalodon teeth are perfect, ready-made tools that could be simply picked up and used. But aesthetics also plays a role: from the beginning of tool-making our ancestors were drawn to beautiful materials. Palaeolithic tools were often made from the most gorgeous stone which had in many cases been traded from afar. And some stone tools even feature fossils—such as the stone axe found in England which has a fossil cockle carefully preserved at its centre. The more I've pondered the teeth of the megalodon, the more I've come to believe that the attraction felt for them by our ancestors goes back to the time when the first stone tools were being fashioned: we may have evolved to love shining, sharp, useful things that fit comfortably in the hand.

So ancient is our attraction to beautiful, useful stones and fossils that our ancestors may even have been picking up fossil teeth of the megalodon while the great shark still

swam in the ocean. Perhaps an *Australopithecus* picked a
tooth from a beach-washed, rotting carcass of one of the last
megalodons. And maybe, just maybe, a megalodon tooth
inspired the earliest hand axes. After all, there's a striking
similarity in shape between the teeth of the great shark
and that of stone hand axes dating back 2.6 million years.
The triangular shape, sharp edge and sturdy hold-fast of
both may merely reflect optimum function. But we cannot
dismiss the possibility that the first hand axe resulted from
fashioning a copy of a megalodon tooth.

There is some, albeit slim, evidence that megalodon
teeth may have been used by non-human species, including
one of our nearest, now-extinct relatives, the hobbit (*Homo
floresiensis*) of Flores Island, Indonesia. These one-metre-tall
upright hominids inhabited a huge cavern on Flores Island
known as Liang Bua, possibly for hundreds of thousands
of years. Several fossil megalodon teeth have been found in
Liang Bua. The limestone that the cave has been eroded
into is Miocene in age, so the teeth may have weathered out
of the limestone as the cave was formed and been redeposited in the sediments of the cave floor. But they may also
have been carried into the cave by hobbits who admired
their beauty and used them as tools.

Abundant archaeological evidence testifies to the idea
that fossil shark teeth have been valued, used and traded by
prehistoric peoples for millennia. For the last 10,000 years

at least, people have found varied uses for fossil shark teeth that go way beyond mere function—as jewellery, protection against various evils, as hunting charms and as tools, to name just a few. The motives of people who have collected fossil shark teeth over the ages can be hard to understand, but the context they have been found in suggests a huge diversity of uses. Use must begin with discovery. What was it that caused someone to pick up a fossil tooth rather than the objects it lay among? Surely the most likely answer is the appeal of the lustrous, jewel-like beauty of a fossil shark tooth's enamel. What makes a jewel? Rarity, lustre, sparkle, colour and shape are all important. Fossilised sharks' teeth possess all of these characteristics to some degree, making them some of nature's most exquisite ready-formed gems. The most seductive are marked with strange patterns in a seemingly infinite palette, from rose blush to blue, yellow, mahogany, white or midnight black. Some fossil teeth are naturally inlaid with golden pyrite or turquoise. And their lustre catches the eye, revealing layer upon layer of shimmering half-seen mysterious shapes as the light plays over their surface. It is perhaps no coincidence that the jeweller Vito Bertucci, who became known as the 'Don of Megalodons', developed a fatal attraction to these fossils. Many beautiful jewels, like the Koh-i-Noor diamond for example, have dark and dangerous histories of people compelled to take enormous risks to get their hands on them.

In some cultures fossilised shark teeth have taken on a religious significance. In pre-Columbian temples across Central America, including in the Mayan city of Palenque in Mexico and Sitio Conte in Panama, for example, fossil shark teeth have been found where they were apparently placed as offerings to the gods hundreds of years ago. And half a world away from Central America in the high mountains of New Guinea, a member of the Mountain Ok group of people used a fossilised shark tooth (probably of the megalodon) along with an ammonite, a fossil bivalve, a gibbsite pebble, and a pelvis and humerus of a tree kangaroo as hunting or gardening charms. These objects were all hidden in a small woven bag the person carried with them. Just how they were used is unclear, but I've seen brightly coloured pebbles kept in a similar bag used as hunting charms by Mountain Ok men who rubbed the charms on the heads of dogs while chanting and performing other rituals to sharpen the dogs' senses.

There's archaeological evidence that for 10,000 years fossil shark teeth have been traded throughout the Americas. Native Americans living in the Chesapeake Bay region were at the heart of the trade, for they lived atop the mother-load of fossil shark teeth—the Miocene-aged Calvert Cliffs Formation, which outcrops on the eastern side of Chesapeake Bay. The people of the area used and modified a great variety of fossil shark teeth to serve as spear tips, arrow points and knives, but they also traded the teeth widely. The teeth of the megalodon travelled as far west as the Ohio River valley, where they became treasured possessions, some even being buried with their owners. At archaeological sites in the eastern USA, a few fossil megalodon teeth have even been found with holes drilled in their roots, suggesting that they were worn as jewellery, kept as curios or had a spiritual value. One such tooth, found in a river in Florida, has a large circular perforation in its root and its serrated edges had been smoothed off, modifications that look very much like it had been used as a pendant.

Australian Aborigines also used megalodon teeth. A farmer once showed me a battered fossil tooth from the lower jaw of a megalodon that he had picked up in an Aboriginal midden of the Gunditjmara people at Buckley's Swamp in western Victoria. The tooth was enormous, weighing at least a kilogram. As the site is many kilometres from the nearest fossil deposit containing fossil megalodon teeth, it must have been carried a considerable distance. I could see by its battered edge that it had been used as a saw or knife. Perhaps the person who picked it up centuries or millennia ago, thought, 'Why make a tool when you can pick up such a fine, ready-made one?'

I would love to know what the Gunditjmara people made of fossil teeth of the megalodon. Did they recognise them as the teeth of sharks or some other creature, or did they believe, as Europeans did until the 18th Century, that they were formed from lightning strikes or other such phenomena? Sadly, much Gunditjmara traditional knowledge about fossils was lost during the horrific massacres of Indigenous peoples by European settlers during the 19th Century, and the long suppression of their culture and language that followed.

On occasion, fossils themselves can tell us something about how Indigenous people viewed them. One of the strangest stories ever told about a fossil, which was probably collected by an Indigenous person, comes from south-eastern Australia. In 1910, a Mr Albin Bishop of Austral Hall, Toowoomba, sold a collection of fossils to the Museum of Victoria for £4. He had assembled the collection on the Darling Downs in south-east Queensland, an area famous for yielding the fossilised bones of many extinct marsupials of Pleistocene and Pliocene times. Many amateur collectors have assembled collections from the sites, and such is the richness of the beds that many museums worldwide have examples collected there. I happened to be volunteering at the Museum of Victoria in 1977 when Tom Rich pulled a jawbone from the specimens sold by Bishop to the museum that looked different from the others. Tom thought that it closely resembled a Miocene species from Victoria. Its preservation looked similar to that of fossils from the Beaumaris site in Port Phillip Bay—the place where I had found my second fossilised megalodon tooth. And it was beautiful—black bone with green teeth. With the help of a microscope, I found the calcareous tube of a tiny marine worm in a crevice in the jaw. On top of the worm was a marine foraminiferan—a tiny creature that lives in the oceans and encrusts rocks and, on occasion, fossils. Similar worms and forams abound in the salt waters of Port Phillip Bay, but they are unknown on the Darling Downs, which is many kilometres inland, on the western side of the Great Dividing Range. The documentation confirming that the jawbone had been collected by Bishop on the Darling Downs in Queensland was undeniable. And research showed that Bishop had never travelled to Victoria, or indeed swapped fossils with anyone. So how could the fossil have got from Victoria to Queensland?

After much puzzlement, our best guess was that the jaw must somehow have got to the Darling Downs from Beaumaris, a distance of around 1500 kilometres, having been carried there by an Aboriginal person who had picked the fossil up at Beaumaris, perhaps thousands of years ago. Perhaps it had been traded from hand to hand as a curio all the way north to the Darling Downs. There, apparently, its journey ended, perhaps because the fossilised jawbones of other giant, extinct marsupials are common on the Darling Downs, so the specimen lost its curio value—a bit like bringing coals to Newcastle. Was it discarded by the dismayed Aboriginal trader and entrepreneur who carried it on the last leg of its journey, only to be picked up, ages later, by the sharp-eyed Bishop? What little evidence we have is at least consistent with such a possibility.

All over the world, fossil shark teeth have been picked up and moved to new locations. Some 5500 years ago, someone—probably a shark hunter—picked up a fossil shark tooth on the Arabian Peninsula in what is now the Sultanate of Oman. The tooth, which was found at the archaeological site of Sharbithat, belongs to *Otodus chubutensis*, the most recent ancestor of the megalodon. It was most likely collected from a nearby fossil deposit, where fragments of 20-million-year-old or older teeth from more than a dozen shark species can still be found today. Tribal peoples involved in shark fishing have lived in the Oman region for more than 8000 years, and they continue to catch sharks for their flesh and oil. They also dry the meat in the hot desert sun to form a kind of shark jerky, for consumption and trade. In their book *Southern Arabia*, published in 1900, Theodore and Mabel Bent described local fishermen hunting for sharks in the surf while riding makeshift sheepskin 'boats' made of two inflated skins joined by a single plank of wood, their legs perilously dangling in the water. The Neolithic ancestors of these people caught large bull sharks (though we don't know how) whose teeth they used as arrowheads. The tooth of a bull shark was found wedged in the vertebra of a Neolithic human body excavated at the site of Ras al Hamra on the Arabian Peninsula. Perhaps it tipped an arrow which was shot into the man, but it also may have been plunged into the man's back by a shark.

European archaeological deposits sometimes yield fossilised teeth of the megalodon. One fine specimen was found in the Pertosa Caves on the slopes of Mount Intagliata near Salerno, Italy, where it had been left by its owner about 5000 years ago. It doesn't appear to have been used as a tool, nor strung on a necklace, and may have been picked as a curio or for use as a charm. And amid the ruins of Jerusalem, one of the oldest cities on Earth, archaeologists have found the teeth of an ancient tiger shark. The twenty-nine 80-million-year-old teeth were buried under the floor of a house almost 3000 years ago, along with some fish food scraps. The fossil teeth bear no wear or puncture marks, suggesting that they were not used as tools or as jewellery. Some archaeologists speculate that they are evidence that fossil collecting was a popular hobby at the time. Whatever the case, we know they were valued because it is likely they had been transported 80 kilometres by horse-drawn cart or on foot. Interestingly, the fossil teeth were found along with hundreds of seals (bullae), which were used to secure important letters and confidential packages. It's possible that the teeth served some role in this process. But it's more likely that someone involved in government or administration had both the education and resources to indulge in the hobby of fossil collecting.

Me, aged 17, with megalodon fossil teeth. The large one was found at the beach at Beaumaris. In my left hand is the fossil seal vertebrae that so interested Dr Tom Rich.

A model set of jaws of a megalodon at the Sharks exhibition, Australian Museum, January 2023.

LEFT: A variety of fossil teeth of adult megalodons from sites across the Americas.

BELOW: Teeth of young or juvenile megalodons from Bone Valley Formation, Florida.

TOP: A Hubbell fossil tooth, from the Bone Valley, Florida.
Hubbell teeth are the teeth a shark is born with.

BOTTOM: A large anterior megalodon fossil tooth from Chile.

A reconstruction of megalodon, approximately 10 times the length of a human.

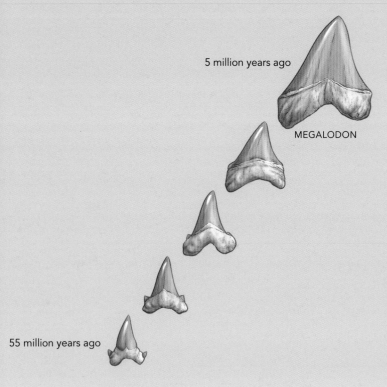

5 million years ago

MEGALODON

55 million years ago

Tooth shape changes over time in the megatooth shark lineage.

CHAPTER 7

The Sweating Teeth of Malta

Fossilised teeth of the megalodon seem to have piqued the interest of the ancient Roman philosopher and natural historian Pliny the Elder, who perished during the eruption of Vesuvius in 79 CE. In his *Naturalis Historia*, which was one of the first scientific encyclopaedias, he speculated that the fossils may have arrived from the heavens as meteorites, and that they had made their way down to Earth during a lunar eclipse. These beliefs circulated in Europe right up until the 17th Century, by which time fossil shark teeth had become the focus of an extraordinary array of beliefs and practices.

Fossil shark teeth are known in Latin as *Glossopetrae*, tongue stones. They were long thought to have magical properties, and between the 13th and 16th Centuries fossils from Malta played a crucial, protective role for some European nobility. The island of Malta is made almost entirely of Miocene limestones and innumerable fossil shark teeth have been found there. Legend had it that they originated when Saint Paul was shipwrecked on the island in 60 CE. Upon landing, so the story goes, the saint was bitten by a viper, and in revenge cursed all of the serpents on the island, punishing them by turning their tongues into stone: fossil shark teeth.

For centuries prodigious numbers of fossil shark teeth were exported from Malta. The 17th Century Danish bishop, anatomist and geologist Nicolas Steno was bewildered that such a small island could produce so many fossil teeth, noting that 'no ship goes thither that does not carry some of them'. The export trade continued for a hundred years or so after Steno's observation, but today the export of fossil shark teeth from Malta is forbidden by law.

Maltese shark teeth were in demand because people believed they could help prevent poisoning, which was in those days a considerable risk for people attending banquets, such as those following marriages or peace agreements, where rivals were obliged to sit together to dine. White arsenic, which looks like sugar powder and can't be detected by taste or smell, was the favoured toxin for such occasions. The Borgia family, which included popes, cardinals and Lucretia Borgia, arguably the world's most

infamous poisoner, became particularly adept at its administration. Consequently, there was a keen market for poison
antidotes and detection kits, and according to the magical
thinking of the day fossil shark teeth were a highly effective means of defence, being able to both detect and neutralise the poison. Before you ate or drank anything at a
banquet, you dipped a fossil shark tooth into your food or
drink, then observed it carefully. If it 'sweated profusely'
or changed colour, it was a sure indication that poison was
about. If any such changes in the fossil tooth were detected,
a second test was administered: a trusted retainer would
taste the dubious food, and he in turn would be closely
observed for symptoms of poisoning. If nothing seemed
amiss, the dish could be cautiously sampled by the banquet-
ers. In the early 17th Century, Michael Heberer von Bretten
left us a firsthand account of such practices. He watched as
guests of the Grand Master of Malta (Head of the Sover-
eign Military Hospitaller Order of Saint John of Jerusalem,
of Rhodes and of Malta) feasted with his guests. One after
another, the guests dipped the proffered fossil shark teeth
into their tankards, before quaffing the contents down. In
those days, it seems, even Grand Masters of holy orders
couldn't be trusted not to poison people. Incidentally, echoes
of this ancient practice may survive today. The custom of
a host sampling the wine prior to serving it to their guests
may not stem, as is commonly assumed, from the host's

desire to test the quality of the wine, but from the tradition of demonstrating that it has not been poisoned.

Shark teeth used for purposes of poison detection were often mounted into elaborate chandelier-like structures known as *Natternzungen-Kredenzen*, which were kept on a small table beside the banqueting bench. Usually made of silver, the presentation of the fossils in such a beautiful structure doubtless boosted the confidence of guests that the banquet about to be enjoyed would not be their last. Just four of these astonishing *Natternzungen-Kredenzen* have survived, and one—a tree-like structure made of silver and precious deep-sea coral incorporating fourteen magnificent megalodon teeth—is preserved in Room 2 of the Treasury of the German Order in Vienna.

The reputation enjoyed by fossil shark teeth as poison detectors grew over time. People came to believe that they could also act as powerful deodorants. This seems to be a rather odd extension of mystical powers, but at the time odours and vapours were considered to be carriers of disease, and if a shark's tooth could neutralise poison, then perhaps it could neutralise odours as well. It makes one wince to imagine the Knights of Malta rubbing their underarms and other delicate parts with serrated, fossil shark teeth and it is hard to imagine them smelling any better afterwards. Yet the magical thinking did not stop there. A belief arose that fossil shark teeth, which were shaped like a horn, were capable of turning aside that most dreaded of curses, the evil eye, which could blight an enemy in innumerable ways. The demand for Maltese shark teeth became insatiable, and fakes soon began to be manufactured. Even the virtuous were seduced by the prospect of profit, it being alleged (though never proved) that the Archbishop of Mainz in Germany became rich through the manufacture of fake 'Maltese tongue-stones'.

Soon all of Europe was awash with fears of fossil fakery, and experts stepped in to provide guidance. The first illustrated book of fossils, published by Swiss polymath Conrad Gessner in 1565, featured a drawing of a fraudulent fossil shark tooth, as well as a method for discerning such fakes from the real thing. According to Gessner, if you worried that you'd been sold a fake fossil shark-tooth poison detector or deodorant, you should wind a thread round the suspect fossil until it was entirely covered up, but without ever doubling the string, and then expose the bundle to a hoar frost. A genuine specimen, Gessner claimed, would get damp, while a fake would stay dry. Alas, the method was useless in places like Malta and much of southern Europe, where poisoning was rife and where the need for deodorants was high, because the weather is too warm for hoar frosts to occur.

As doubts crept in, some worked at sorting fossil shark teeth into those that were good at detecting poison, and those that were not. A good shark tooth, it was claimed, had a shiny surface, was odourless and tasteless when masticated (which was doubtless a tooth-breaking exercise) and would carbonise before being reduced to ashes in a fire. The 17th Century Danish natural historian Ole Worm was sceptical about the fire test. He and others pointed out that, if a good fossil tooth was subjected to such a test, it would then be useless for detecting poison, on account of it having been reduced to a charcoal-like substance.

Malta is a densely populated island, yet fossil teeth of the megalodon can still be found there. As late as the 1970s they remained abundant enough that concentrations of them could be searched out from afar with binoculars. Sir David Attenborough would visit his friend Desmond Morris, who lived in Malta at that time, and soon became obsessed with the search. He would bring his family with him on holiday (though his daughter Susan confided to me that, due to the search for shark teeth, these were really 'working holidays'). David would sit in his deck chair on Morris's patio, scanning the surrounding valley walls through his binoculars. He was searching for a particular layer of sediment rich in nodules, at the base of which lay a concentration of fossil shark teeth. Below the fossil-rich layer was a layer of rock soft enough to be eroded by the wind. This allowed caves to form, into which fell concentrations of fossils. Once he spotted a suitable cave, David and his children would traipse through fields, vineyards and scrublands until they reached the cavity. If it was shallow, David would reach in and gently excavate the fossil teeth. If not, a member of the family would have to crawl in.

In 2022 Sir David showed me his collection of fossilised megalodon teeth from Malta. It consisted of dozens of magnificent specimens, all well curated and labelled. He told me a curious story. In 2021, for Prince George's eighth birthday, Sir David gave him one of the teeth from his collection, in the hope that it might trigger an interest in palaeontology. This act of generosity was reported by the media, and soon after he received a letter from an official of the Maltese government, expressing outrage that Sir David had stolen such an important part of Malta's patrimony, and demanding the immediate return of the specimen. Sir David quite rightly replied that he had collected the tooth decades before any law preventing their export had been passed. In fact, had Sir David not collected the teeth they would by now be dust, having been destroyed by wind, rain and erosion. I think that the rather overzealous official who penned the letter owes an apology!

Perhaps the last word on this curious episode of the use of fossil shark teeth should go to the fossils themselves, in the form of Johan Reiskius' poem, written in 1684. It's a

play on the old name 'tongue-stone', and is written from
the perspective of a Maltese shark's tooth:

> To speak like a stone or a rocky tongue, I cannot.
>   Yet I speak with young women, young men and
> old men, and speak in tongues.

By the time of the Danish natural historian Ole Worm
in the 17th Century, the world was entering the era of
rational scientific inquisition, and the study of fossil shark
teeth offered an excellent way of investigating what fossils actually were. In 1666, a major breakthrough occurred.
Danish anatomist, geologist and later bishop, Nicholas
Steno, who was personal physician to the Medicis and then
living in Florence, was brought the head of an enormous
female great white shark that fishermen had caught off the
coast of Livorno, Italy. The creature had been dragged on
shore, tied to a tree and savagely battered to death, so the
carcass was not in great shape. Nevertheless, Duke Ferdinand II ordered that it be carried to Steno in Florence for
examination. The duke might have been motivated by an
interest in the opinion of the Medici's personal physician
regarding the efficacy of fossil shark teeth as detectors of
poisoned food, the Medicis being no amateurs in the use
of white arsenic. Whatever the case, only the head made it
to Florence and it must have been well-rotted by the time
Steno got his hands on it. Undeterred, the great anatomist

dissected it, and in 1667 published a comprehensive account of his findings.

Steno compared the teeth of the shark to strikingly similar fossils that were common in the coastal hills near the site of its capture. It seemed implausible to him that fishermen had been capturing giant sharks and distributing their teeth over the Tuscan hills in such numbers as to account for the fossils. He thought that the teeth found inland were very old, and that they had weathered out of the rocks. This key insight would eventually lead to the science of stratigraphy—the study and meaning of rock layers.

While Steno may not have been the first to identify the organic origin of fossil shark teeth, he was the first to provide an explanation for how such fossils came about. Initially he was baffled by how one solid object (a fossil) could be embedded in another solid object (the surrounding rock) and proposed that rocks had once been fluid (indeed a sedimentary layer begins as a slurry). He correctly noted that fossils are found only in layered sedimentary rocks that are the petrified remains of an ancient sea floor. Today geologists think of Steno as one of the founders of their science, and his ideas form the basis of geological teachings in schools and universities. Interestingly, we may soon have to speak of Saint Nicolas. In 1988 he was proclaimed 'beatus', the third of four steps required to attain sainthood in the Catholic Church. Many Catholic students of geology continue to pray at his tomb for exceptional exam results. He only needs one more certified miracle to become a full saint.

About the time Steno published his landmark study, he began losing interest in science and turned increasingly towards a religious life. Such was his devotion that Pope Innocent X ordained him as the Titular Bishop of Titiopolis (a bishop in title only as the 'titular' of his title indicates). Titiopolis was a town in south-western Turkey that had been abandoned almost 1000 years earlier, yet the Catholic Church continued to appoint bishops to look after its non-existent population. Being a bishop helped ease the way for Steno's scientific publication, despite the fact that it implied a great age for the Earth and so contradicted biblical teachings. His book, whose title translates as *Concerning a Solid Body Enclosed by Process of Nature Within a Solid*, was eventually passed by the papal censors, and following its publication in 1669 became widely available.

By the early 19th Century the church was losing influence, and the science of palaeontology was becoming established in infant form. Some of the greatest minds of the age were being drawn to the mystery of the megalodon. In 1806 Thomas Jefferson donated a fossil tooth of the species, which had been found at Rice Hope Estate on the Cooper River in South Carolina (a site that continues to yield megalodon teeth to this day), to the collections of the

Academy of Natural Sciences in Philadelphia. It bears the number '959' putting it among the first thousand specimens registered in that venerable institution in a collection that today comprises millions. Just what Jefferson made of the fossil is not clear, but it is accompanied by the label 'Tooth of a Leviathan'.

It fell to the Swiss scientist Louis Agassiz, born in 1807, to name the great shark. Agassiz was one of the greatest scientists of his age and is acknowledged as the first person to recognise that the Earth had been through an ice age. He was also one of the world's first experts on fossil fish: between 1833 and 1843 he published a five-volume compendium on fish fossils, in which he named a new species of shark *Carcharodon megalodon* (later changed to *Otodus megalodon*) 'the great, sharp tooth'. Most of the fossil teeth Agassiz used in describing his new species were drawn from museum collections. Sadly almost all lacked precise locality data, except one, which was documented as coming from Malta. Agassiz seems to have been in awe of the fossil teeth he described and named, saying that they 'excite a keen interest . . . because of the frightening portrait they paint in our minds'. He was convinced that his new-found species of shark dwarfed all living types, though just how large the megalodon was he could not determine.

Palaeontology has developed tremendously since Agassiz's day. Now, globe-straddling teams of researchers peer into fossils in ways Agassiz could never have imagined. During the last 150 years we have learned an enormous amount about the megalodon. We have defined its distribution and are gradually zeroing in on the time of its extinction. We have learned about its means of reproduction, its diet and growth rate. But many mysteries remain, including its maximum size—which so puzzled Agassiz. While computers may assist us in informed speculations about the great shark's proportions, it is only by wearing out more shoe leather in the search for more complete fossils that a definitive answer to this longstanding puzzle will be found. And because there are just not enough palaeontologists in the world to conduct the search, amateur fossil collectors will continue to play an important role. Thankfully, some of these amateurs are as single-minded and dedicated to the search as any professional, and are willing to work closely with museums to document and preserve their finds. This is all part of the growing field of citizen science, which is amplifying effort and accelerating discovery in many fields of science the world over.

CHAPTER 8

The Don of Megalodons

At about 2.30 pm on Sunday 17 October 2004, Vito Bertucci, a fit, handsomely moustachioed 47-year-old jeweller from Port Royal, Beaufort County, South Carolina, slipped into the dark, turbulent waters of the Ogeechee River in Georgia. It was a bad day for diving. A 2.5-metre current was running and, according to a veteran scuba diver who knew the area well, entering the water would be like chasing 'the Atlantic Ocean up a wall ten feet high'. Bertucci, who was loaded down with more than 60 kilograms of weights and equipment, was headed for a deep hole in the river bottom, which had been found earlier by diver Terry Lee. Lee had been chased out of the hole by bull sharks, but that didn't deter Bertucci. He had a good feeling about the place. And he felt up to the challenge presented by the turbulent waters. He was the most experienced fossil shark-tooth-hunter of his times, and he'd explored many deep holes before. This hole, he thought, was just the kind of place—so deep, dark and forbidding that it had remained unexplored—that might yield a treasure trove.

By 5 pm that day Bertucci had failed to return to his boat, and his partner raised the alarm. The rescue team sent to search for Bertucci embarked on an exhausting five-day marathon in water so dark, according to one rescue diver, that 'you can't see anything except what's underneath your light on your belly'. Despite the efforts of the rescue team, Vito Bertucci was not seen until he surfaced a week later, in Ossabaw Sound, Chatham County. The dive had cost him his life but, as Vito anticipated, the deep hole had indeed been filled with treasure, as attested to by the bag full of fossil shark teeth that was found strapped to his body.

We don't know what happened in that deep, dark hole that day, but having dived for megalodon teeth myself I can imagine Bertucci's last moments. Feeling for the big megs in the muddy bottom, his fingers would have encountered one sharp blade after another. Picking them with mounting excitement and tucking them into his collecting bag, maybe he was so exhilarated that he'd missed the warning signs of nitrogen narcosis, a condition that can drive you mad. Perhaps in his delirium he imagined that he was picking the teeth from the maw of the great shark itself. Or maybe he was in his right mind, and had got tangled in a lost fishing net, or trapped under a sunken log, where he struggled until his air ran out. Or maybe the titanic battle with the current, or a brush with a bull shark, caused a heart attack. Whatever killed the Don of Megalodons, the world should mourn his passing, for few have contributed more to the collection of the physical evidence left behind by the great shark.

Master dive-trainer Ralph Neeley said that he would never have gone diving in the current that flowed on the day of Bertucci's death, much less into a black hole. So what compelled Vito to take the risk? Perhaps he overestimated his abilities. But overriding everything surely was his passion for megalodon teeth. Vito Bertucci was obsessed with them, and I can testify as to how all-consuming that passion can be. 'You couldn't talk to him about anything but sharks' teeth,' recalled John Woods, a collector based in Savannah, Georgia. 'That was his life.' Barker, a friend of Bertucci's, agreed. 'You could say it's a nice day—it led to sharks' teeth. You could say your mother died—it led to sharks' teeth. All roads with Vito Bertucci led to sharks' teeth.'

Bertucci sold most of the teeth he found. A sales pitch for one find, which was over 18 centimetres long, read: 'To locate the tooth, and hundreds of smaller ones like it, Bertucci had to battle tiger and bull sharks, alligators, cotton-mouth snakes, sea wasps (jellyfish) which can carry fatal stings . . . all in water that is usually pitch black and filled with strong currents.' Though a hyperbolic, compressed account of the dangers Bertucci encountered while diving, the excitement conveyed of the chase is not too wide of the truth.

Vito Bertucci was born in 1956—the same year I was—and I sometimes think, 'There but for the grace of God go I.' With the Don gone, his discoveries remain as testimony to his obsession. Foremost among them is his reconstruction of the jaws of a megalodon containing 182 fossil teeth recovered throughout twenty years of diving by Vito himself. They must come from many individual sharks, so the jaws are a composite. The largest four teeth are 18 centimetres long, putting them among the largest megalodon teeth ever found. Few fossil collectors will ever find a tooth this size, and the fact that Vito found at least four is a monument to his labours. The reconstructed jaws are nearly three metres high and almost 3.4 metres wide—so capacious that a man can stand inside them and still have plenty of headroom. Scaling the jaws to the best length estimates we have, suggests that they represent a shark that was about 23 metres long. Bertucci's reconstruction is not strictly scientifically accurate, and nor should we expect it to be, as Vito was not a scientist. But what it reveals with frightening clarity is how Vito saw the great shark that so obsessed him.

I look on those jaws as a terrible manifestation of the fact that the monster that was the megalodon is still with us. Indeed, it has grown since its extinction, becoming an outsized emblem of all the unspoken, hidden terrors that haunt our imaginations. For Vito Bertucci the megalodon was an oversized presence and, akin to Ahab's obsession with Moby Dick, it would eventually drive Vito Bertucci to his death.

Despite having become extinct millions of years ago, the megalodon still kills an average of two people a year. Its victims are mostly divers like Vito Bertucci, drawn to search for the treasure of the deep. And as the easy fossils are found, divers venture into ever deeper, more dangerous waters. Above all, the deep, dark and deadly holes of the USA's east-coast waterways continue to lure them, for it's rumoured that there, enormous fossil teeth remain so abundant that they form dense pavements to these pits of hell.

Not all of those drawn into the search for the fossilised teeth of the megalodon face such dangers. But whether they look for treasure on land or at sea, the world of the fossil megalodon tooth hunter is one of rip-roaring adventure. Palaeontologists too have adventures aplenty in their work, but they also enjoy well-informed and mind-bending imaginary time travel at the same time as solving profound scientific mysteries. The lives of jewellers and those who buy their fossils to augment their collections may seem more sedate, yet they too enjoy their armchair adventures. Driven by an appreciation of the unique beauty of megalodon teeth, they seek the perfect specimen at mineral and fossil shows, or online, always hopeful of a bargain price.

CHAPTER 9

Where the Beautiful Megs Lie

A superb, fossilised tooth of the megalodon is a feast for the eye, the mind and a wonder to touch. Enamel as smooth as silk, in any colour from jet black to blue, violet, mahogany or white, a serrated edge as sharp as a samurai sword, and a heft of more than a kilogram. The great triangle of enamel in your hand was once alive. It moved through the sea at the pointy end of the greatest predator that ever existed, and it shredded the flesh of the fiercest prey. It is the process of fossilisation that has transformed a tooth dropped from a rapacious mouth into this thing of beauty, and the unique conditions under which these processes occur that make each fossil tooth distinct.

Many factors influence the character of a fossilised megalodon tooth, and each fossil locality yields teeth of a particular quality and colour. Local variations in sediment and groundwater flow mean that even teeth from the same locality can differ greatly in appearance. The colours depend largely on the nature of the sediment that the megalodon tooth was preserved in. But the geochemistry that colours the teeth is so specific that even on a single tooth, each part can display a different colour. Some crowns, for example, are grey with blood red cutting edges. Others are bright green and marked with bizarre black shapes, while others can be mottled with milky white and eggshell blue. This variation occurs because as the groundwater leaches minerals into fossils, cracks and other flaws act as conduits for the dissolved minerals, so concentrating them.

The hobby of collecting megalodon teeth boomed in popularity after the 1990s with the advent of online auction sites such as eBay. Before then, collectors had to attend rock and mineral shows or go to specialist shops to purchase specimens. Buying fossils is always a gamble, if only because it's always possible that an abundant trove of even better specimens will be discovered, devaluing your investment. Despite this gamblers' thrill, buying a megalodon tooth is surely the tamest way to acquire one. It's far more fun to find your own. The hunt adds considerably to the appeal of collecting and personalises your collection. It also provides an element of surprise. In some parts of the world, particularly in the eastern USA, you can come across fossilised megalodon teeth almost anywhere. Building sites, drains, quarries, beaches and roadsides have all yielded spectacular finds. Little wonder that collecting fossil shark teeth has become an all-consuming passion for some. Occasionally, the find of a big meg looks just too good to be true. I once purchased a modest-sized megalodon tooth that had been picked up by a diver in shallow water off a sandy, popular swimming beach in Florida. It had a repaired chip in the root, and when I enquired about it, the diver confessed that when he first saw it lying in the sand, it looked so perfect that he assumed it was a fake fossil, or piece of jewellery that had been dropped by a swimmer. To test his idea, he bashed it with a hammer!

The many fossil localities on the east coast of the US that yield megalodon teeth are scattered all the way from Florida to Maryland. They are varied in the nature of the exposure of the sediments yielding the fossils, with rich deposits on land, in rivers and at sea. Access to some (particularly quarry sites) is strictly forbidden, but many are open to the public. The best time to search, particularly in rivers and on beaches, is after floods and storms, events that can move vast volumes of sediments, exposing fossils.

It's important to understand that an abundance of fossils does not necessarily mean a past abundance of sharks.

Some places are fossil hotspots simply because fossils are accessible, or have been concentrated there by wind, water or human activity: the spoil heaps of quarries, pebble banks and deep holes in riverbeds. Such areas can become picked over, however, forcing serious fossil hunters further afield. In North Carolina, divers descend 30 metres in clear Gulf Stream waters to unearth monstrous megalodon teeth nestled in mere centimetres of sediment. During the last ice age 20,000 years ago, when seas were 120 metres lower than they are today, parts of what is now North Carolina's continental shelf were riverbeds. The flowing rivers eroded the teeth out of the older sediments and concentrated them in potholes in the stream floor. Then the ocean rose, drowning the rivers and the fossil shark teeth. Indeed, the abundance of megalodon teeth in North Carolina is such that the state has designated the megalodon tooth its official fossil emblem.

Adjacent states, however, are hardly lacking in superb megalodon collecting localities. Around Summerville, South Carolina, for example, fossils can be found on land, embedded in super-soft sediments very close to the surface. The teeth originate from the Chandler Bridge Formation, which crops out in rivers, creeks, building sites and other places around the town of Summerville. Fossil megalodon teeth are often exposed after heavy rains in this area, and if you're in the right spot at the right time, you can pick them up from the muddy ground, sometimes as many as tens of teeth in a week. Occasionally megalodon teeth wash up on South Carolina's beaches as well, as Xander Buck could tell you. Xander was only five and on holiday in 2021 at a resort near Myrtle Beach, South Carolina, when he bent down and retrieved an eight-centimetre-long tooth from the mud exposed at low tide. Myrtle Beach must be a lucky spot for five-year-olds, because just a couple of months earlier Brayden Drew, also five, found a glorious black tooth the size of his palm in the shallows—at the very same location.

Nine-year-olds can be lucky as well. Molly Sampson and her younger sister Natalie had been bitten by the fossil-hunting bug, and both asked for insulated chest waders as Christmas presents so that they could search shallow waters for fossils without getting wet. On Christmas Day Molly asked to be taken to Calvert Beach, Maryland, to put her waders to work. She wanted to go fossil hunting, she said, 'like a professional'. She was in knee-deep water when she saw a promising shape. She dove in to retrieve it, and came up sodden, but with a near-perfect, 13-centimetre-long, bottle-green megalodon tooth in her hands. It was, one curator said, 'a once in a lifetime kind of find'. But I've got a feeling that Molly is so inspired by the discovery that she'll continue to make spectacular finds for many years to come.

Across North America, the precise sites that yield the best fossil megalodon teeth are often tightly guarded secrets. Some locations, however, have become so famous that they cannot be concealed. The Aurora phosphate mine in North Carolina produces some of the most beautiful fossil shark teeth to be found anywhere on Earth. Indeed, some like to imagine that Aurora is the fossil-hunting capital of the world. The fossil megalodon teeth found there have a haunting beauty, their background colour often a milky white, mottled with eggshell blue. The bourlette (the band between the root and the crown on the rear face), in contrast, is often patterned in complex meanderings of mahogany and black, while the root is tan or whitish. Few very large teeth are found at Aurora, but what Aurora teeth lack in size, they more than make up for in charisma.

The Aurora mine used to have an association with the Friends of the Aurora Fossil Museum, and twice a year the lucky museum friends were allowed onto the mine site to look for fossils. Sadly, the mine is now closed to fossil collecting, and I suspect that many beautiful and informative fossils, which might otherwise have been retrieved and treasured, are now ground to dust for their phosphate content, to be strewn across crops!

The Aurora Fossil Museum continues to host an annual fossil festival, however, replete with fireworks and live music, which often features a fundraising auction of a large megalodon tooth. A giant heap of sediment, called the Pit of the Pungo (named for the Pungo River Formation, a layer of sediments that yields the fossils), is dumped outside the museum for the occasion, attracting enthusiasts who can search through it for their own fossils.

The Bone Valley Formation in central Florida also yields exquisite fossil shark teeth. Like the Aurora mine, very few large specimens are found here (supporting the hypothesis that the area was a nursery ground), but the Bone Valley teeth are so extraordinary in colour and pres- ervation that they are my favourites. In fact, Bone Valley is unique in producing fossil teeth of every colour, from pur- est white to jet black. Some layers in the deposit yield teeth whose enamel is daffodil yellow, while others are eggshell blue, or dark blue, or green, or brown speckled with black. Some have colourful patterns stained into the enamel; oth- ers have black or white bourlettes; yet others have roots that contrast in colour with the bourlette and crown.

Most of the fossil megalodon teeth found in Bone Valley are from very young sharks, and the smallest teeth found there have a distinctive heart-shape. Known as Hubbell teeth, they are thought by some to have been the teeth that great sharks were born with. The only way we'll ever know for sure is if a whole-body fossil of a pregnant megalodon is found. But it is an awesome feeling to hold and contem- plate such a tooth, imagining it being used in the dark of the womb for the terrifying purpose of devouring foetal siblings.

Bone Valley is one of the most prolific fossil deposits in all of North America—the Florida Museum of Natural History alone houses more than 27,000 fossils of cartilaginous fish recovered from the Bone Valley Formation. Exposure of the fossil-bearing layers often occurs through mining, for Bone Valley is located in the Central Florida Phosphate District—a huge region pockmarked with mines, where machines inevitably grind up thousands of fossils for fertiliser. Access to the mines is generally forbidden, but many people hunt for fossil shark teeth in the shallow creeks that wind through the remaining forests between the mines. Some walk road verges, searching for teeth of the great shark among the road metal dug from the mines and used to resurface roads. Possessed by the fossil fever, they defy the peril of errant trucks, or stand all day and night metre deep in cold water, shovelling gravelly sludge that they call 'gravioli' into sifters, hoping to find 'the big one'. I know fossil hunters so obsessed with this activity that they've worn their hips out as they agitate their sieves, and have had to have them surgically replaced.

A dealer who sells megalodon teeth online told me he sourced most of his stock from people who live in trailer parks. His contacts enjoy diving in rivers, he said, and sell whatever they find for beer money. In Georgia and states northwards, there are a few people who make a decent living from diving for megalodon teeth. Bill Eberlein, a rescue-and-recovery diver in the freezing waters of Lake Erie, began searching for shipwrecks in the lake, before moving to Georgia for the more tropical water. Someone told him about the fossil shark teeth that are to be found in the waters off Richmond Hill, and he was quickly infected with the fossil fever. Bill says that he isn't too bothered by diving in the zero-visibility conditions that prevail in the area, but he tries not to think too much about the things he bumps into, or that bump into him, as he plunges down through the murk and debris. His most prized find is 'The Beast', a 17.6-centimetre-long megalodon tooth, which is kept in a safety deposit box. It has been valued at more than US$15,000, not that Bill would contemplate selling it. But he does sell about a thousand lesser teeth a year through his website. His list of customers is extensive and speaks eloquently of the variety of people who collect fossil shark teeth—from American doctors to British Lords. He even uses fossil megalodon teeth to pay his dentist for services rendered.

The blackwater rivers of North Carolina produce relatively few megalodon teeth, but those found are highly prized. They are a rich mahogany colour, having been stained by the low-oxygen, acidic and iron-rich waters. Blackwater rivers are usually slow-flowing and they pick up their distinctive colour as they pass through forested areas, the tannins from the vegetation darkening the water.

With visibility quickly diminishing to zero, and with lots
of slime-covered logs, branches and other debris to get
trapped under, diving in blackwater rivers must be one of
the most risky and terrifying ways to become the owner of
a fossil megalodon tooth. And it takes persistence in the
face of such constant terror, with finds sporadic and few
or no areas offering a concentration of fossils. Yet the dis-
coverers of such gorgeous teeth would argue that the risks
are worth taking, even for a small chance of obtaining a
blackwater river tooth. The Meherrin River in Hertford
County, North Carolina has produced some of the most
exquisite blackwater teeth of all. They typically have hand-
some chestnut enamel and reddish-brown roots, as do many
of the teeth from the blackwaters near Franklin, Virginia.
The occurrence of teeth there is, however, very localised,
with long stretches of potentially deadly river entirely bar-
ren of fossil shark teeth.

More than 200 years ago the murky brown waters of
the Cooper River in South Carolina yielded a megalodon
tooth to Thomas Jefferson. It was probably found on the
riverbank, possibly by the great man himself. Today finds
in such accessible places are rare, but the river continues to
attract its share of daring, fossil-hunting divers. The experience is reported to be confronting. Once submerged, it is
impossible to see more than half a metre in front of you. If
you peer towards your feet you are met with nothing but

a turbid expanse and, due to the strong currents, divers must weigh themselves down heavily to avoid being swept away. As the water rages around them, they pull themselves towards the riverbed with a rope attached to an anchor, and in the gloomy water the rope is soon their only point of reference. Once they reach the bottom, a torch is required, as well as a spike to pull themselves along, and a small rake to trawl through the gravelly substrate. As with fishing, fossil hunting requires patience. It must be difficult to concentrate in such perilous circumstances, yet divers spend hours, day after day searching the same location, hoping to feel that smooth enamel of a shark tooth with their probing fingers.

Away from the east coast of the USA, the distribution of fossil megalodon teeth is more patchy. There are highly productive sites in California, including the famous Sharks Tooth Hill locality near Bakersfield, a tiny area on private property containing a breathtaking density of fossils, where access is strictly controlled. Megalodon teeth also turn up occasionally in Europe—on beaches in Belgium and the Netherlands, for example, and in limestone quarries in France, Spain and Italy. A tooth has even been found in Romania. And of course there is Malta, with its storied and highly protected abundance of fossil megalodon teeth.

In the UK megalodon teeth can occasionally be found along the Naze cliffs on the Essex coast. In 2019 brother

and sister Adam and Sophie Pollard made the news after
stumbling across a gigantic, heavily weathered specimen
that is estimated to have come from an 18-metre-long giant.
In 2021, at least two more megalodon teeth were found
by those cliffs by members of the public, one of which is
so well preserved that some suspect that it is a fossil from
North Carolina that had been planted at Naze as a ruse!
And the finds continue, with six-year-old Sammy Shelton
finding a magnificent tooth there in May 2022. It is truly
remarkable, incidentally, how many splendid megalodon
teeth have been found by young children. Doubtless being
close to the ground, having razor-sharp vision, and a mind
open to all possibilities are great assets when you're looking
for fossils, and six-year-olds have all that in spades. If you're
interested in searching for megalodon teeth at Naze, it's
important to know that the cliffs are prone to collapses, that
the area is protected, and that excavation is prohibited. The
best place to search for megalodon teeth is on the beach,
which is permitted and occasionally productive. If you do
get lucky, please alert the local park authorities. They will
make a scientifically important record of your find—but
won't take it from you!

In the 1990s the island of New Caledonia became an
unlikely source of megalodon teeth, when people began
dredging up bucket-loads of teeth from waters more than
300 metres deep. Most of the teeth were deeply corroded

after long exposure on the sea floor, but they were truly abundant, a single dredge-pull lasting 30 minutes sometimes containing hundreds of teeth. The discovery tells us that the megalodon cruised the waters off New Caledonia. Today, humpback whales travel seasonally to the same warm waters, so perhaps in times past megalodons fed on whales that followed a similar route. Sellers of New Caledonian megalodon teeth often try to enhance the looks of damaged specimens by carving and staining their surfaces with scrimshaw-style designs. This I think is a disfigurement. A megalodon tooth in its unaltered state is a magnificent thing and far too precious to deface by carving.

The discovery of a megalodon tooth in Australia is now an extremely rare event, with most potential fossil sites concentrated in Victoria. Most of the localities that have yielded such fossils in the past are now exhausted. But recently, a number of magnificent specimens turned up at an unexpected locality in Port Phillip Bay, virtually in the suburbs of Melbourne. The locality is of great scientific importance, so its precise whereabouts cannot be revealed. Were the deposit to be plundered by fossil collectors, rather than being carefully and methodically excavated and recorded, a huge amount of scientific information would be lost forever. The odd tooth has also been found in moderately deep water off Flinders Island in Bass Strait. Cape Range National Park, near Exmouth in Western Australia, has also yielded specimens. This isolated, coastal range is made up of limestone from an ancient sea floor, and in places it is littered with adult megalodon teeth. Like the New Caledonia locality, the Cape Range region lies today at the end of a migration route for humpback whales, so perhaps this area was also once a seasonal hunting ground for megalodons. It's difficult to extricate the Cape Range teeth from their surrounding limestone, which is extremely hard, and it can take up to a year in a laboratory for acid to dissolve the rock surrounding each tooth. The taking of anything (including fossils) from a national park is strictly forbidden but, sadly, thieves have stolen teeth from the Cape Range. In 2018 they poached a specimen that was almost 10 centimetres long from a secret location there. Word of the occurrence of large specimens of teeth of the megalodon can spread like wildfire, making it very difficult to protect specimens left in the rock. Before the tooth at Cape Range was stolen, park officials had attempted to conceal it with vegetation and rocks and had even contemplated enclosing it in bullet-proof glass. Alas, the proposed measures came too late.

South America is something of a holy grail for those interested in the teeth of the megalodon. The largest tooth ever found was 19 centimetres long, and was discovered in the desert at Ocucaje, Peru. Today this tooth is held in a private collection. It's possible other, even larger teeth are hidden away in other private collections. One of the largest and most beautiful megalodon teeth I've seen is a privately owned specimen that was reputedly found in a cart-rut in a track in Peru. Peru strictly prohibits the export of teeth of the great shark, which is a good thing as fossil deposits like the Pisco Formation, where they are found, have the potential to yield a huge amount of scientific information that might increase our understanding of the megalodon if they are properly excavated. A priceless heritage would be quickly devastated if wholesale, non-scientific fossil-collecting were permitted. Fossil smugglers are known to frequent Ocucaje, and occasionally police intercept stolen cargos of large fossils, such as whale skulls, hidden in places such as the holds of buses. To prevent such priceless items being poached, palaeontologists often disguise their discoveries, as it can take weeks to dig them out and recover them without damaging them.

The colours of megalodon teeth from Peru vary enormously, with some a gorgeous violet colour. Very rarely they are whitish-pink, and covered in tiny circles, each of which encloses a dark dot like a miniature bullseye. Others are green, or tan. Just why such astonishing colours and patterns have formed on teeth from Peru is not known. Another characteristic of some Peruvian megalodon teeth is that they are hydroscopic, absorbing moisture from the atmosphere due to their salt content. This can cause them to appear to 'sweat', as moisture is attracted to them, just like the supposedly poison-detecting fossil shark teeth from Malta. For those interested in explaining the myth, it would be worth investigating whether Maltese shark teeth are also hydroscopic.

In 2018 fossil megalodon teeth from West Java began to appear for sale online. Two years later, they were flooding the market, advertised at prices well below those of equivalent quality teeth from elsewhere. This resulted in a rapid drop in the price of megalodon teeth globally, destroying the illusion promoted by many sellers that fossil shark teeth might be a profitable, long-term investment. Today, fossil shark teeth have never been cheaper, and such is the richness of the Indonesian deposits that low prices may persist long into the future. The Javanese teeth are dug out of the sediment by local people using picks and shovels, and so the deposits have come to support something of a cottage industry. This is good for the local economy, though the cost of the practice to science has yet to be estimated. On Java, the sale of the fossils is a venerable tradition—possibly going right back to the discovery of the so-called Java Man fossils in East Java in the late 19th Century.

The Java Man bones—which consist of a skull cap, thigh bone and tooth—were excavated from the banks of the Solo River in 1891–92, through the extraordinary efforts of Dutch palaeoanthropologist and geologist Eugène

Dubois. Dubois was a medical doctor and academic who became convinced that humans originated in the East. He abandoned his academic career and joined the Dutch army so that he could be posted to Indonesia, where for eight years he searched for fossils of what he called the 'missing link'. He found his El Dorado near the village of Trinil in East Java, and in 1891 published the discovery of what he called 'a species between humans and apes'. Hugely controversial at the time, the bones, which are about 500,000 years old, are now classified as *Homo erectus*, a species immediately preceding *Homo sapiens*. Tragically, few researchers at the time recognised the significance of Dubois' finds, and the mental torture of having his life work ignored had a severe impact on him. Increasingly embittered and secretive, Dubois refused to allow anyone to examine his fossils. By the time he died in 1940, he was largely forgotten, and was buried in unhallowed ground, in an anonymous grave at Venlo in the Netherlands.

Fossils of many kinds continue to be found along the Solo River in Java. Lines carved into the shells of freshwater mussels found at the site were recently hailed as the world's oldest art. Villagers have long searched for fossils there and they sell whatever they find to foreign visitors, many of whom are interested in the palaeontology and geology of the historic site. A vigorous trade in all sorts of fossils was thriving when I visited the Sangiran area in the early 1990s. I had travelled from the nearby city of Solo by becak (a three-wheeled motorised passenger vehicle), and as I got out, hoping to examine the fossil beds, a crowd gathered and thrust sundry fossils and other curios at me. Among them were the fossilised molars of extinct hippos, Javan rhinos and gaur, the native cattle of Java. The cries of the vendors were deafening, and although I spoke pretty good Indonesian, it was difficult to understand what was being said. I didn't want to buy fossils, and I tried to explain that I just wanted to see the historic fossil site, but the crowd of sellers would have none of it. They were intent on making a sale and seemed to take my reluctance to buy as evidence that I was holding out for something special.

After a few minutes the crowd quieted, then parted. A gentleman stepped forward and surreptitiously drew an object from inside his coat. It was a small black skull, and as he presented it, he whispered that it was Java Man himself! Judging by its size, I quipped that it must have been the skull of Java Man when he was a boy. But the object was so strange that I asked for a closer look, at which the vendor rather reluctantly passed it to me for examination, whispering the price as he did so, '*Juta rupiah*' (a million rupiah). The object was clearly made of fossilised bone, but upon examining it closely, I saw that what I had taken to be a skull was in fact only a remarkably accurate carving of a skull, which had been fashioned from the head of the femur of an extinct elephant.

The crowd was expectant, the seller clearly an important person. I was in a difficult situation. An allegation that the skull was a fake might have caused umbrage, and things could have quickly turned ugly. After thinking for a few moments, I said that I couldn't possibly buy such a precious object of Indonesian heritage, if only because I'd never get permission to export it. I then added, *sotto voce*, that if, however, the skull was a fake, it might be possible for me to buy it, and to get an export permit. At this the vendor became highly agitated. I thought for a moment that he might admit to its fakery, but he mustered his courage and instead insisted that this was the one and only true skull of Java Man. There was nothing more to be said. Seeing that I would not buy, the man tucked the carving back into his coat and turned away. By this time I had given up on seeing the fossil deposits, and as I hopped back in my becak and headed for town, the owner of the alleged Java Man skull stalked off, doubtless looking for a more gullible buyer.

The fossilised teeth of the megalodon coming out of Indonesia today are excavated from sediments that outcrop east of Trinil. But I wonder if the fossil entrepreneurs I met in the 1990s have become involved in the fossil shark tooth trade. Many of the teeth advertised for sale online have been cleverly repaired, and even 'improved', by various artifices that require at least as much skill as that required to carve a hunk of fossil elephant femur into a skull. Perhaps my old friend, the owner of the 'Java Man' skull, has chosen an easier sell, and switched enhancing megalodon specimens for the shark tooth trade.

CHAPTER 10

Shark Eats Man

The most haunting of our imagined monsters remain hidden as they stalk us, striking when we least suspect it, while we are relaxing, or at play. The megalodon roams the ocean unseen and unseeable, except in our imaginations. And it often surfaces in our consciousness when we are at rest or play by the seaside. The reason that the great shark holds such a chilling grip on us must be sought in the very long history of the interaction of sharks with people. Is there anything more spine-chilling than the thought of being eaten alive? Tigers and crocodiles occasionally eat people, but they are restricted to specific regions that are far removed from the areas inhabited by the majority of humans. Of all the great predators, only sharks patrol the waters off all our coastal cities and tourist resorts. As with the most feared of monsters, they are the ever-present, unseeable terror.

There is a contentious theory that our species went through an aquatic phase during its evolution, according to which the long periods our ancestors spent in the sea foraging for marine life account for our hairlessness, our thick layer of subcutaneous fat, and our abilities to swim and hold our breath. If the theory is true, then perhaps this primeval foray into the water has something to do with our deep fear of submerged predators.

More certain is the idea that at least 50,000 years ago, people were making heroic oceanic voyages, for example, to reach Australia. In those days, well before the widespread despoilation of the oceans, these first intrepid mariners must have crossed waters that often roiled with sharks and their prey. Perhaps they even lost the odd companion to snapping cartilaginous jaws. Whatever the case, as soon as our ancestors began plunging into the sea to travel or to exploit it for food, they exposed themselves to the risk of encountering sharks.

Archaeological excavations have provided some convincing evidence that sharks have preyed on humans for many millennia. In 2021 researchers announced the unearthing of the skeleton of a shark-attack victim in a Japanese cemetery that was almost 3000 years old. The unfortunate person was most likely a fisherman, and his bones bore almost 800 marks made by serrated teeth—most likely from a tiger shark or a great white. The marks included deep incisions, punctures, striations and cuts, and by mapping them on a three-dimensional model, researchers were able to tell that the victim was alive when attacked. One of his hands was cleanly sawn off, possibly the result of a desperate attempt to break free from the predator. And both legs had been severed from the torso in the attack, one of which had been placed upside down on the corpse prior to its burial. As gruesome as the find is, we are fortunate indeed to have such evidence of prehistoric shark attack, first because buried shark-attack victims must surely be in the minority, as the bodies of many victims are never recovered, and second because it's rare even for a buried body to remain intact for 3000 years.

Over time, many human communities have struck a balance between fear and respect for sharks, and in some of the most ocean-going cultures of the world, both humans and sharks thrived. Because sharks play vital roles in the marine ecosystems, this live and let live association facilitates healthy, stable food chains, which bring real benefits to humans as well as to the environment.

Many of the communities that maintain a respectful relationship with sharks have incorporated the creatures into creation myths as ancestors, or gods. In Maori mythology Parata is the shark-god who lives in the depths of the ocean. With each breath he controls the oscillation of the tides. The Fijian shark-god Dakuwaqa is the protector of fishermen, shielding them from the jaws of sharks and securing their safety at sea. Sharks can be attracted to canoes and can even swim ahead of them in ways that make it appear that they are guiding the humans in the vessel, and of course, sharks know where the best fishing grounds are, all of which may have influenced Fijian beliefs.

In Hawaii it was believed that the ancestors could manifest in the form of a shark, and that sharks would guide canoes and herd fish into nets. In the Solomon Islands, sharks steer the transition from the living to the spirit world. There, bodies of the dead are laid on reefs at low tide, to be eaten by sharks, allowing the spirits of the deceased to join the ancestors. On Anaa Atoll in the Tuamotu Archipelago, warriors take the name of the oceanic whitetip shark, and in large areas of Polynesia sharks that live in the open ocean (some of which are known man-eaters) are seen as taboo and cannot be killed or eaten.

In some traditional Polynesian societies, sharks even provided a spectacle. In a strange parallel to the Colosseum contests of ancient Rome, 'volunteer' Hawaiian warriors would sometimes engage in battles to the death against a shark. The spectacle occurred in a sea pen, fashioned with large basaltic rocks. Bait was placed inside to lure sharks into a narrow opening that faced the open ocean, and once a shark was in the pen, the opening was closed and the warrior plunged into the water, brandishing a small wooden rod that terminated in a single shark's tooth. As the shark lunged at the warrior, he would aim the tooth-dagger toward the beast's belly in a bid to disembowel it. Human victories were rare, and the few men who did survive gained great *Mana* (prestige) and were believed to have gained supernatural powers.

Following the adoption of Christianity in Oceania in the early 1800s, many of the beliefs protecting sharks broke down, and some previously protected species were intensively fished to the point that they vanished from the once well-frequented waters. Only in the most remote and uninhabited of places, such as Caroline Island in Kiribati, or the privately owned Clipperton Island, can the full glory of sharks before human hunting decimated them now be appreciated. In a spectacle reminiscent of the Pacific before human exploitation, hundreds of black-tipped reef sharks can be seen in the lagoon shallows there, while numerous larger sharks patrol offshore. All are so unafraid that they will bite at the paddles of rowers making for the shore, and even nip at their feet as they wade onto the beach.

The oceanic whitetip is a deep-water species of shark that has been severely impacted by the breakdown of pre-Christian taboos that protected it. It's a slow-moving, slow-growing species with a low reproductive rate, and as it was killed in increasing numbers by newly minted Christians it went into swift decline. One favoured method was to travel far out to sea and to use a goat as a lure. When the oceanic whitetips approached, the fishermen would lasso the sharks by the tail, one by one, as they approached the bait.

As Europeans embarked upon the age of sail, voyaging to evermore distant parts of the globe, they encountered predatory sharks, in many cases for the first time. Early English voyagers referred to them as sea-dogs, but eventually the term shark, derived from the Dutch word for scoundrel, was adopted. The spectacle of both a shark attack and a heroic rescue is eerily yet beautifully conveyed in a 1778 painting by John Singleton Copley, 'Watson and the Shark', held in the National Gallery of Art in Washington, DC. It depicts a ghastly event that occurred in the 1740s, when 14-year-old orphan Brook Watson imprudently dived off a small boat he was working on in Havana Harbour, Cuba. Within view of several horrified onlookers, a panicked Watson was dragged underwater by a huge shark that had latched on to his leg. He resurfaced once, only to be pulled under again by the shark. A crew member finally chased the shark away with a pole topped with a large hook. The creature left bearing Watson's right foot and onlookers were able to rescue the lad. Amazingly, Watson lived to tell the tale. In Copley's painting

Watson floats naked in the turbulent waters, his body pale and vulnerable, one arm desperately outstretched to several men in a boat, as the monstrous shark approaches with its jaws wide open.

Australia is world-renowned for its shark attacks, and while a number of attention-grabbing attacks by great white sharks have occurred in recent years, records of encounters with various shark species go back to the very first European explorations of the continent. Shark Bay in Western Australia is renowned for its enormous tiger sharks. Their powerful jaws are able to crack the shell of a sea turtle with ease, and the creatures have a fearsome reputation for eating anything they can get their jaws around, including the most indigestible of garbage. Their ferocity was made plain by Francois Peron, the zoologist on the Baudin Expedition, who in 1801 wrote:

> The eastern side of Fauré Island [in Shark Bay] is infested with sharks remarkable for their size and voracity. One of these monsters almost devoured Lefevre, who had saved my life in the Josephine Islands. He was already knocked over: the terrible shark was about to swallow him, when three other sailors running up at his shouts managed to rescue him from the jaws of the animal. Furious at thus being deprived of its prey, the shark hurled itself

several times at a sailor, succeeding in tearing off
part of his clothing, and only retired when it had
received five wounds.

Such brazen attacks are extremely rare today, yet they
abound in the annals of early Australian exploration. It's
hard to avoid the conclusion that either large sharks have
become much rarer, or more cautious, over the years.

In October 1805, just 17 years after the first British out-
post was established in Port Jackson, some of Australia's
earliest European settlers watched as a huge shark attacked
an Eora man who was fishing in the harbour in a bark
canoe. The shark repeatedly rammed the canoe, attempting
to capsize the frail vessel. The fisherman made for the shore
as fast as his spoon-shaped paddles would allow him, with
the shark in swift pursuit. All the while he was distracting
the shark by throwing, one by one, the small fish he had
caught into the water. He reached the shore just as the last
of his fish was disposed of and declared in amazement that
another 'ten yards must have sacrificed him'.

In Sydney's early days domestic dogs were frequently
carried off by sharks. The situation was not improved when
slaughterhouses were established around the harbour and
the offal disposed of into the water. Yet neither sharks nor
pollution put off some swimmers: in the 1830s one hardy
fellow was seen swimming naked except for a top hat,

while smoking a cigar, in the waters off Woolloomooloo. He remarked to onlookers that he regularly swam there and didn't fear the sharks. Others were not as fortunate. In 1837, on the MacLeay River about 450 kilometres north of Sydney, a particularly horrifying attack took place. A 12-year-old boy was washing his feet in the shallows when he was seized by a large shark. A tug of war began when a man who was nearby tried to pull the boy from the predator's mouth. The boy was finally freed, but the shark then pursued both man and boy to the very edge of the water. Sadly, the boy died shortly afterwards.

Today, the USA records the greatest annual number of shark attacks (with Australia the second). Yet shark attacks were almost unknown in the USA during the 19th Century. Historian Jennifer Martin notes that sharks were regarded by many North Americans as fearsome-looking yet benign creatures that had no desire for human flesh. Indeed, the idea of a shark attacking anyone was considered so absurd that in 1891 Hermann Oelrichs, a multimillionaire American businessman, offered $500 to any person who could prove that a swimmer had ever been attacked by a shark. The reward, at the time a substantial sum, was never claimed.

It was not until 1916, as the result of an infamous spate of attacks off New Jersey, that Americans' views about sharks changed. The attacks took place over twelve days in the hot summer of that year, and they triggered fear and panic across the country. The first victim was bitten by a shark while swimming with his dog close to a beachfront hotel. Most of the flesh was stripped off one leg. He was dragged from the water by onlookers and into the foyer of the hotel, where he bled to death. A mere five days later a shark struck again. This time the victim was a Swiss hotel attendant who had arrived in America just weeks earlier. Switzerland is landlocked, so at the time the Swiss were generally not familiar with the danger posed by sharks. The young man was enjoying an afternoon swim about a hundred metres offshore when he was spotted crying out for help. He was twice pulled under, disappearing each time with a splash, and each time he was submerged one of his legs was bitten clean off. Severely mutilated, he barely made it to shore before expiring.

A week later a 10-year-old boy was swimming with friends in Matawan Creek, New Jersey, when he was attacked by a shark. Several locals arrived to help, and a man bravely entered the water to retrieve the boy's body. He reached the corpse, but in front of a crowd of horrified onlookers, he too was fatally attacked. Frustrated and full of fear, locals bombed the creek with dynamite.

Why so many attacks occurred over such a short period of time, in such a small area, is not known. It was not until the early 1900s that ocean swimming became commonplace, so perhaps the combination of a hot summer with more people taking a dip in the sea, along with a healthy shark population, had something to do with it. And while exceedingly uncommon, it is possible that an individual shark might have been responsible. Matawan Creek is wide and deep, and at the time of the attacks it was high tide on a full moon, conditions more than welcoming for a great white. And, interestingly, a great white with human remains in its stomach was caught not long after this spate of attacks.

Great white sharks, the largest living predatory fish on Earth, are responsible for a third to a half of all fatal shark attacks. But the risk of death from attack by any shark is very small—around 1 in 3.7 million. That is minute when compared with the risk of being shot and killed in the USA (which in 2020 was about 16 in 100,000) or being killed in a car accident. Great white sharks are found in the world's cooler waters, and radio tracking has revealed that they often migrate long distances, from Australia to South Africa and back for example, a distance of 20,000 kilometres. Their streamlined torpedo-shaped body is built for speed, and for short bursts they can reach speeds upwards of 50 kilometres an hour. Humans aren't their preferred prey. Younger great whites feast on fish and other sharks, while adults more commonly turn their teeth to turtles, seals and dolphins. It is young great white sharks that are more often than not implicated in attacks on humans, perhaps because as adolescents they are inquisitive and inclined to experiment with what they can eat. In any case, some scientists speculate that most attacks on humans are cases of mistaken identity, as the silhouette of a swimmer or surfer is all but indistinguishable from a seal to a great white patrolling below. Giving credence to the premise that humans are not often actively sought out by great whites is the fact that non-aggressive close encounters between great white sharks and surfers or paddle-boarders are more common than once realised. Footage of such interactions is today often caught by drones and posted on the internet, with the perilously close human none the wiser.

The tiger shark and bull shark hold second and third place respectively in recorded human bite frequency. The fact that both tiger and bull sharks are at home in the shallow waters of bays and estuaries, where humans like to swim and play, may account for the high number of attacks, as might their size, curiosity and aggressiveness. After the great white, the tiger shark is the second-largest predatory shark. It is named for the faint stripes that are present on its back as a juvenile. Great whites and tiger sharks are easy to tell apart: the great white has a pointy nose, while that of the tiger is wide and blunt. Although tiger sharks prefer warm tropical waters, their habitat overlaps with the cool-water-loving great white and the two were implicated in the simultaneous attack and death of a 57-year-old male swimmer off Perth in Western Australia in 2021.

For many, the shark that instils the most fear is the stout and pugnacious bull shark, not least because it ventures into waterways one might expect to be shark-free. Bull sharks are one of the only shark species able to tolerate brackish and even fresh river waters, and they are known to travel great distances into turbid estuaries. Bull sharks have been caught in the Mississippi River, 1200 kilometres inland from the Gulf of Mexico, and some have been spotted in the Amazon River, an incredible 4200 kilometres inland. The species possesses several physiological adaptations that allow it to do this. Like all sharks, bull sharks must maintain a sufficient internal concentration of salt to prevent cell death, and they achieve this via their kidneys, which recycle salt. They also recover some salt from their food with their atrophied rectal glands.

Bull sharks can be extremely territorial and will attack in very shallow water, as scientist and conservationist Erich Ritter discovered. While filming a program for the Discovery Channel in the Bahamas in 2002, Erich was bitten on the left calf by a large bull shark. He was standing in only about a metre of water, and the shark bumped Erich with its head before attacking, a common occurrence reported by people who have been bitten by bull sharks. Gory footage following the attack shows Erich being carried out of the shallows by his rescuers in a pool of his own blood, skin hanging down like drapes over the missing muscle of his calf. Ironically, the segment Ritter was filming was presenting the notion that bull sharks have been unfairly characterised as aggressive.

Given the frequent proximity of bull sharks and people in warm, shallow waters like harbours and estuaries, attacks are astonishingly rare. And not all shark attacks in such areas can be attributed to bull sharks. One tragic attack, by a bronze whaler shark, occurred at Parramatta, at the head of Sydney Harbour, on 26 February 1996. It was late at night and Darren Good had been egged on by friends to dive into the water with a bet that he didn't have the guts do it. His pride hurt, Darren dived in and won the bet. Shortly after entering the water, however, he was bitten on the right testicle, and then left leg, leaving him in considerable pain and distress. Perhaps the shark had mistaken him for a large fish.

Sometimes it is not the shark that is the suspect in a human killing, but rather the informant. In 1935 Bert Hobson snared a four-metre-long tiger shark while fishing with his son off Coogee Beach, Sydney. Hobson transported the shark alive to the nearby aquarium, which he owned, in the hope it would drum up business. For almost a week the creature swam contentedly in its exhibit, until on Anzac Day, 25 April, it took a turn for the worse. Being a public holiday, the aquarium was busy, and many people peered through the glass to get a glimpse of the ferocious predator. After seeming to be disoriented and listless, it suddenly vomited up its entire stomach contents, causing the watching public to recoil, for floating in the foul-smelling discharge was a half-digested rat, a bird, and a tattooed human arm. When the arm was examined by a pathologist, it turned out that it had been cleanly severed from the body with a knife.

The local newspaper published details of the tattoo to help identify the deceased. As a result the police were contacted by one Edwin Smith, who had been searching for his missing brother, Jim, for several weeks. Jim owned a local billiards bar and was known to engage in various illicit activities, including fraud, forgery and cocaine smuggling. Businessman Reginald Holmes, who had employed Jim in various felonious plots, was quickly identified as a prime suspect. After hearing that the police were after him, Reginald attempted suicide on a boat in Sydney Harbour. He survived the single shot to his forehead, only to be found dead several weeks later, his corpse riddled with bullets, at Dawes Point under the Harbour Bridge. He had been killed just prior to the opening of the inquest into Smith's death, and some speculated that he organised his own demise via hitmen, so as not to besmirch his reputation or void his life insurance, which would go to his family.

Whatever the case, before his death Holmes named accomplice Patrick Brady as Jim's murderer. Patrick was charged but eventually acquitted, largely due to the fact the single arm recovered was not proof enough for the judge that poor Jim was in fact dead!

World War II cemented the ugly reputation of sharks as man-eaters. In 1945 the sinking of USS *Indianapolis* by a Japanese submarine led to what remains the worst tragedy in America's naval history. The vessel was carrying just under 1200 men when, not long after midnight on 6 August, it was hit by torpedoes. Almost 300 sailors lost their lives as stored aviation fuel ignited, causing deafening explosions and huge flames that stretched high into the air. The ship had been catastrophically damaged, and in less than a quarter of an hour was on a journey to the sea floor. Floating and exposed in the vastness of the ocean, the surviving men watched as slow-moving oceanic whitetip sharks began to maul the bobbing dead. When the corpses ran out, they turned on the injured, and when they were all consumed, the sharks began on the rest. The men floated in groups, desperate to protect themselves from the feeding frenzy. But even the opening of rations, such as a can of spam, caused the arrival of countless sharks attracted by the smell of meat. Many men who survived the initial sinking of USS *Indianapolis* died from shark attack, and even more died from exposure, in the four days before they were rescued. Only 317 traumatised men lived to tell the tale.

Oceanic whitetips have been menacing seafarers for centuries, if not millennia. They spend most of their lives far from the continental shelf, in deep water but close to the surface. As they glide through the ocean with their paddle-like pectoral fins they are perpetually on the lookout for their next meal. Being opportunistic predators, they will eat almost anything that smells like food. Imagine all the canoes and ships that have ever sunk in the open ocean over the long maritime history of our species. Before too long, many of those hapless sailors would have been surrounded by the hungry mouths of oceanic whitetips. Though the vast majority of whitetip attacks remain unrecorded, this shark is probably responsible for more human deaths than any other species.

Several years prior to the USS *Indianapolis* incident, the US Navy undertook an extensive investigation into shark-deterrent devices. The most promising invention they found was the 'Shark Chaser', a chemical repellent that was doled out to US Navy officers for decades. Subsequent studies, however, showed that it was completely ineffective. Unsurprisingly, shark deterrents have been experimented with by various cultures for centuries. The Aztec people of central America took to suspending chilli peppers from the sterns of their canoes while fishing, in an attempt to repel sharks.

The use of capsaicin (the component in chilli responsible for the burning sensation) was recently tested as a shark deterrent on the TV show *MythBusters*. Balloons filled with capsaicin paste were submerged in the ocean near bait boxes. Curious sharks burst these balloons with their sharp teeth, resulting in clouds of intense chilli in the water, but neither the sharks, nor nearby fish, were repelled by the capsaicin.

Through the 1960s, as the US media continued to highlight shark attacks that occurred in American waters even though they were very occasional, authorities resorted to some spectacular methods. In one instance, following a supposed close call (perhaps it was only a shark sighting) near Coney Island, the local newspaper reported that the police fired machine guns into the water. A rather breathless article in a local newspaper followed, replete with photographic evidence. While no doubt satisfying nervous members of the public, spraying the waters with machine-gun bullets must be the most ineffective means of protecting people from sharks ever tried. Today fishers and surfers continue to use a range of shark-deterrent devices and concoctions, from machines that project a strong electrical field to magnetic and olfactory deterrents. While some of these are effective in certain circumstances, attacks continue.

The long experience of the people who live with sharks shows that the best defence against shark attack is to know your marine environment and the sharks that inhabit it.

Knowledge of shark habits, for example, allows divers in places like Beqa Lagoon, Fiji, to dive with enormous predatory sharks without being attacked. So respected are the sharks that the reef the dives occur on was proclaimed a protected area in 2004—possibly the first marine reserve to protect large predatory sharks anywhere in the world.

Sensationalist media reporting of shark attacks was doubtless a driver for the success of the book and subsequent film *Jaws*. The film franchise was a huge success, with no less than three sequels produced, each of which depicted mindless, man-eating sharks mauling helpless swimmers. Australian diver, conservationist and filmmaker Valerie Taylor was commissioned to work on the set of *Jaws*, alongside her husband Ron. Throughout her life Valerie has been on her own personal shark-focused journey, from competitive spearfishing shark-killer in the 1950s to fierce protector of sharks in recent years. As a highly experienced diver, she is very much at home in the deep blue and, although 87 at the time of writing, she still keeps the company of sharks, being recently filmed in her bright pink wetsuit surrounded by sharks in Fiji.

For the making of the film *Jaws*, Steven Spielberg required a mechanical shark 'prop' more than 7.5 metres long, and 3000 kilograms in weight. Most large adult great whites are about five to six metres long and weigh 1000 kilograms, so Spielberg's prop was oversize for a great white

shark. Indeed, it was within the size range of the megalodon itself (albeit at the small end). When filming scenes
with real-life great white sharks off South Australia the
film crew used a half-size diving cage, and had intended
hiring a midget to get into it, to give the impression the
surrounding great whites were larger than they in fact
were. Thankfully, they found a stunt man of small stature
instead. Carl Rizzo was an ex-jockey who, at just 1.5 metres
tall, was almost perfect for the job. Unfortunately, he had
little diving experience and lacked Valerie Taylor's love of
sharks. He also seems to have been largely uninformed
about some of the more challenging aspects of his role.
When asked to enter the scaled-down shark cage while an
enormous great white shark prowled nearby, Carl hesitated,
and in doing so he probably saved his life. As he stood on
the deck equivocating, the great white became entangled in
the ropes holding the cage, wrenching the entire apparatus
free and sending it to the bottom. After seeing the mayhem
Carl, quite understandably, locked himself in the boat's toilet. It's a credit to him that, after he had calmed down, he
went on with the job.

Jaws was released in 1975, and it immediately fuelled
an increase in the killing of large sharks, mainly by fishers hoping to secure trophies such as jaws, teeth and even
entire bodies. On occasion, such trophies have been transformed into works of art. Damien Hirst's 1991 'The

Physical Impossibility of Death in the Mind of Someone Living' consists of the body, preserved in formaldehyde, of a 4.3-metre-long tiger shark that was caught off Queensland. It last sold for somewhere between US$8–12 million. The success of the work inspired Hirst to create similar pieces, including 'Immortal' which features a preserved great white shark, 'Death Denied' (a shark carcass split in two lengthwise) and 'Leviathan' (a preserved basking shark). These works blur the lines between art, museum taxidermy and sportsroom trophies.

Sharks are far slower to reproduce than many bony fish. Having few young, they are unable to replenish their populations as quickly as humans can decimate them. Tragically the peak of trophy hunting could not have come at a worse time, coinciding with a dramatic reduction in food sources for the great white shark. Populations of seals and whales had crashed due to industrial-scale human hunting, and by the 1970s many previously abundant seal and cetacean species were on the brink of extinction.

The psychology of trophy hunters reflects the ethos of an era that is, I hope, swiftly passing, one in which humans are seen as pitted against nature, rather than being part of it. Perhaps western society was misguidedly searching for a reason to conquer the frightening beast, to take back the power that sharks seem to have over us, at least when we enter their realm. Instead of preserving carcasses in formaldehyde, the urgent need is to preserve the last of the great living predators, so that stability and productivity can be brought back to ecosystems.

Over the longer term, the impact of the movie *Jaws* has led to some positive environmental outcomes, including an increasing awareness of and interest in sharks. This has led to more research that has underlined the case for conservation. One such study, published in 2010, estimated that the total worldwide adult population of great whites was only 3500—far lower than was previously thought. Australia, which records the second-highest number of shark attacks of any country, had already moved to protect great white sharks in 1999, and successful prosecutions have occurred under the legislation, including of a fisher who killed a juvenile great white on the south coast of New South Wales in 2012. He was fined $18,000.

Since a spate of shark attacks in 1935, a number of popular swimming beaches in Australia have been protected by shark netting. The nets do not entirely enclose a beach. Rather, segments of net are sunk four metres below the surface, entangling sharks and other passing marine megafauna. The killing of the otherwise protected great white sharks in such nets is allowed under existing legislation, but opposition to the nets is growing. Since the inception of the program, it's estimated that 19,000 large marine creatures have been killed by the nets, including turtles, dugongs, dolphins, whales and non-target shark species. There is no doubt that the nets are effective in protecting swimmers, with very few attacks being recorded at netted beaches. But in 2021, six out of the eight local council areas in New South Wales whose beaches are protected with nets requested that the state government remove them and provide alternative protection.

Even as shark attacks have increased in Australia attitudes towards the harming of sharks continues to change. This is reflected in the sentiments of families who have lost a member to shark attack, some of whom plead with authorities not to harm the shark that killed their loved one. When Western Australian surfer Brad Smith was taken by a shark in 2004, the ABC reported: 'Authorities Monday continued to hunt for the killer shark and said they would likely shoot it if they can conclusively prove they have found the animal responsible for Smith's death.' But the shark found an unlikely ally in the dead surfer's brother. 'I don't believe that the shark should be killed just for the sake of what's happened in this situation,' Stephen Smith told reporters. 'I don't believe that Brad can be revenged by killing a shark.'

This is not an isolated incident. Rob Alter is a Western Australian surfer who has lost two mates to sharks, in one instance pulling the body of the victim from the water himself. In commenting on attempts by the Western Australian government to kill sharks that might attack swimmers, Alter said: 'The government can't legislate away risk, they simply cannot do it . . . As a surfer I know it is a risk, but it is a risk that I choose to take when I go into the water. To the government—please don't interfere with my right to experience the ocean in its natural, wild state. If I wanted something controlled, I'd swim in a pool.'

Rob's attitude is in fact close to that of the traditional cultures of Australia and the Pacific, where dangerous creatures are feared but also revered and protected. And his views are reflective of a wider Australian trend. Australians have become used to living with many types of dangerous creatures, and many people now appreciate that if nature and humans are to coexist, accommodations need to be made. Perhaps the closest historical parallel for the evolving tolerance of Australians towards sharks is found in the changing views of saltwater crocodiles, which are the largest and most dangerous reptile on Earth. Prior to their protection in the early 1970s they had been hunted almost to extinction, and Australians had become used to camping, swimming, kayaking and fishing pretty much wherever they wanted around tropical waterways. Some even took to sleeping in crocodile habitat. As crocodile numbers recovered, however, a series of ghoulish attacks occurred, including the killing and carrying off of people who were camped beside a river some distance from the water. Governments responded with greater signage and awareness programs, as well as the targeted removal of large crocodiles (which were transferred to crocodile farms) in the vicinity of popular camping spots. As people altered their habits, attacks abated. Today, crocodiles are more abundant than ever. Tourism in crocodile-infested regions is increasing and crocodiles and humans manage to co-exist, with a greatly reduced incidence of fatal attacks.

CHAPTER 11

Man Eats Shark

There is much horror in the idea of being eaten by a shark. Yet sharks are responsible for only about ten human deaths a year, and in most of these cases the victim is bitten, but not consumed. Humans, in contrast, kill about 100 million sharks a year. That's three sharks killed every second of every day. Many of these sharks are eaten by us. Consequently, it's estimated that the total number of sharks has halved in the past 50 years.

Shark-hunting has a venerable tradition that long predates the development of modern industrial methods that are now devastating shark populations. In hunter-gatherer archaeological sites from pre-colonial Brazil, shark teeth are found in their thousands. The teeth and vertebrae of more than 15 species, including such fearsome sharks as the great white and tiger, occur there. The majority of the remains from some species are from juvenile sharks, and it is likely they were hunted in nursery areas after being herded to shallow water. Shark teeth are often found in ash layers, suggesting the sharks had been cooked, and leading researchers to conclude that Brazilian Indigenous peoples had been eating sharks for hundreds, if not thousands of years, and that sharks comprised about 50 per cent of their diet. Isotopic analysis of human remains confirms that the Indigenous Brazilians occupied a similar ecological position to the megalodon—both were super-predators getting much of their food by eating other predators, principally sharks.

Ethnographic accounts made about 500 years ago in the Americas detail an extraordinary hunting technique that may have been used to obtain larger sharks. It involves cornering the shark and enticing it to attack. As soon as it opens its mouth, its throat is speared with a sharp stick. An even more extraordinary technique was documented by Ferdinand, son of Christopher Columbus, who in the late 1400s described the use of a remora as a living fishing hook by the inhabitants of Cuba. The remora is an odd-looking, elongate fish with a sucker on the top of its head that can form a bond so sturdy that the remora remains attached to a shark or a dolphin, even as its host leaps into the air. *Remora* means 'delay' in Latin, and the fish got their name because their presence was (falsely) thought to slow down ships. Most remora consume the faeces of their host, and some species will plunge deep into the cloaca of a shark in search of food. Ferdinand Columbus describes how the Cuban fishers tied a strong fishing line around a remora's tail, plopped it in the ocean and waited for it to adhere itself to a fish, shark or even turtle. After it had fastened on, the remora was pulled towards the boat and the catch hauled out of the water. This method has also been documented among fishers in east Africa, north-eastern Australia, and south-east Arabia.

The Catholic Church bears some responsibility for the widespread consumption of sharks. I was brought up as a Catholic, and as a child I unknowingly ate shark every Friday. One of our observances (originally instituted because a pope owned extensive fisheries and wanted to increase fish sales) was to eat fish, but no other meat, each Friday. I grew up in Melbourne, where the cheapest fish at the time was sold under the commercial name of 'flake'. Flake could be the flesh of any shark, but most of it came from the gummy shark. This species is unusual among sharks in that it grows fast and breeds prolifically. Because of this, and the fact that the gummy shark fishery is one of the best regulated shark fisheries in the world, it's considered

to be sustainable—a notable exception among the world's
shark fisheries. But I fear that much of the 'flake' I ate as
a child was sourced from other, less quickly replenished
shark species.

Surely one of the least sustainable fisheries ever to exist
involved the taking of the slow-growing and long-lived
Greenland shark. Between the 19th Century and the 1960s,
this species supported a small-scale fishery, with as many
as 30,000 individuals taken per year. Because the shark is
so long-lived (up to 440 years), the impact of the fishery
will be evident in the age structure of the living population
for centuries to come. The flesh of the Greenland shark
has a high concentration of trimethylamine oxide, which
makes it toxic and causes it to reek of urine. To render it
edible, fillets must be buried for six to eight weeks in frigid
soil, allowing the meat to ferment, after which it is hung
to dry for six months. The half-rotten flesh that results is
known in Iceland as *hákarl*. It's definitely an acquired taste,
stinking of ammonia and having a weird texture. Celebrity
chef Anthony Bourdain said of *hákarl* that it was 'the single
worst, most disgusting and terrible tasting thing' he'd ever
put in his mouth. Others have likened it to chewing on a
urine-soaked mattress.

It's not just fisheries targeting sharks that are devastating shark populations. Other kinds of fisheries, especially
those using long lines of baited hooks to catch swordfish,

tuna and mackerel, can catch more sharks than fish, and the sharks caught almost inevitably end up dying. According to the UN's Food and Agriculture Organisation, there are few fisheries that don't accidentally catch at least some sharks. Non-target species caught in such fisheries are known as by-catch. Often they can't be sold, so are wasted. Precise estimates are hard to come by, but overall, it seems likely that the impact on sharks resulting from by-catch is substantial, with tens of millions of sharks dying this way each year.

The impact of fisheries for shark meat and by-catch are sadly dwarfed by a single specialised industry—that providing the ingredients of shark-fin soup. An estimated 73 million sharks are caught each year just for their fins. The fishery is particularly cruel and wasteful, with living sharks being hauled into a boat to have their fins sliced off. They are then discarded, alive, into the sea, where they drown or are eaten by other sea creatures, and the dried fins are shipped to market. Shark-fin soup is considered a luxury or high-status food in China and other parts of east Asia. A particular kind of cartilage found in shark fins, called ceratotrichia is its key ingredient. To make soup the fins are shredded and boiled. The fin itself is tasteless and devoid of nutrients, but it imparts a much-valued gelatinous texture to the dish.

Shark fin is also an element in traditional Chinese medicine, believed to enhance sexual potency and the appearance of the skin, as well as to help cure heart disease. The reality, however, is that shark fin can have high levels of the neurotoxin BMAA, as well as mercury, which is a neurotoxin that is particularly dangerous to pregnant women and unborn babies. Thankfully, the popularity of shark-fin soup seems to have peaked around 2000 in China. There is still a market for it, however, in China and elsewhere, though substitutes are now often used.

Biologist David Shiffman made the interesting point that if the megalodon were found alive today it would likely not be long before it faced extinction due to the shark-fin trade. He calculated that the fins of a single adult megalodon could sell for upwards of $600,000 and would produce 70,000 bowls of shark-fin soup. That's enough to feed the entire population of Greenland, with enough left over for half to come back for seconds!

CHAPTER 12

The Imaginary Meg

My daughter, Emma, first saw the movie *Jaws* when she was six years old. She was far too young to be exposed to such a terrifying story, and the viewing came at a particularly bad moment in our lives. Earlier the same day our house had burned down in a bushfire, and some neighbours had kindly offered to put us up in their house. I was exhausted from fighting the fires and promptly fell asleep. But Emma and my son, David, then eight years old, were invited to watch a movie with our host's children, who were a few years older. I had no idea that, after such a traumatic day, Emma and David would be exposed to the spectacle of an unrelenting predatory shark on a mission to destroy human life. Whether it was her age, the circumstances of the day, or just the sheer terror of the film, *Jaws* had an enormous impact on Emma, leaving her in equal measure both fascinated by and terrified of sharks.

For weeks Emma was terrified to go to the toilet. She said that the light in the bathroom cast shadows like a shark's jaws, and that a shark might lunge up from the bowl. Even after our house was rebuilt she remained haunted by her fear, to the extent that she felt that swimming in our backyard pool was fraught with danger. As she dived down, she found the tick, tick, tick sound of the pool cleaner eerily similar to the two-note theme of the *Jaws* score. With every dive into the pool, she says, her heart pounded, and she was unable to stop imagining the razor-sharp teeth of a great white approaching. Her fear soon became an obsession. Although now in her 30s, she still suffers from recurring dreams in which a giant shark lunges out of the shallows and encloses her in its jaws.

Peter Benchley, the author of the novel *Jaws*, on which the film was based, regretted the negative impact that his work had on the public perception of sharks. In the last decades of his life (he died in 2006) he wrote a number of non-fiction books about sharks in an effort to better inform the public about their reality. He also became a strong advocate for marine conservation. After his death, his family established the Peter Benchley Ocean Awards to further his conservation work.

Spielberg made *Jaws* a brilliant representation of attitudes to sharks as they were before the rise of environmental conservation. The human characters are complex, embodying attitudes we can instantly empathise with, as well as being startlingly vivid. The shark protagonist of the story is, in contrast, so one-dimensional it might as well be a robotic killing machine. We humans have always filled our imaginations with monsters, the best of which are complex beings—a bit like us—and very unlike the one-dimensional shark featured in *Jaws*. Grendel, the monster from the Anglo-Saxon poem *Beowulf*, is a great example of the kind of complex terror I'm talking about. He starts out as a bit of a stereotype, but then we meet his mother, who cares for him in their underwater lair after his arm is ripped from its socket by the poem's hero Beowulf. Seeing family love among monsters provides a more complex, satisfying story. It tells us that Grendel is not alone, but part of a family. The terror will live beyond his death. And of course, the strong bonds of love between mother and son provide an extra edge to our fear of how Grendel's mother might react when her son dies.

When Louis Agassiz described the megalodon in the early 19th Century, it possessed, in his imagination at least, some of the mystery that a truly haunting monster requires.

But these days, courtesy of *Jaws* and its sequels and imitations, the megalodon is all too often reduced to a mindless, ravening killer—a parody of a shark. We can surmise, based on the behaviour of living sharks, that the megalodon, the greatest shark of all, which was a living, thinking, feeling being, which bred, navigated and communicated as well as killed. It almost certainly had its own social structure, its own awareness of its place in the world.

The power that the megalodon continues to exert on our imaginations is such that we cannot let the beast lie. It continues to manifest in all sorts of human creations, from movies to books and internet discussion groups. In each one it takes on a different form, and a different purpose. The 2018 film *The Meg* marks, perhaps, the awful apogee of the great shark as a one-dimensional, murderous monster. The movie's plot involves the discovery of a relict population of great sharks that has been hiding out for millions of years in the deepest parts of the ocean, under a thermocline (a boundary between warmer and cooler water) with hydrogen sulphide. Below, the great shark, along with a variety of long-lost deep-sea fauna, thrive in isolation—until they are discovered by a submersible which is sent to rescue the crew of a crippled nuclear submarine that has sunk in the Marianas Trench.

In Hollywood style the submersible is attacked by an enormous megalodon, which then escapes the thermocline by following the submersible to the surface. The giant shark then roams the high seas, causing havoc, until it is wounded and, in a form of poetic justice beloved of Hollywood, is eaten alive by other sharks. The film ends with speculation about whether just one, or several megalodons have escaped the thermocline, opening the door to the possibility of a sequel. *The Meg 2*, its website says, is slated for release in August 2023.

For those who want to believe that the megalodon survives, the ocean deep is the obvious refuge. Internet chat forums, where people discuss evidence for the species' survival, invariably involve the deep sea. Some believe that the intense water pressure of the abyss would not be a problem for the megalodon, on the implausible basis that 'being a shark, the sea "flows through them" since they don't have lungs, but gills'. Other participants explain that the megalodon could very well live in the deep sea in waters of reasonable temperature, as long as it sticks close to hydrothermal vents. But the thermal gradients at hydrothermal vents are very steep. Just a few metres from a vent the water can be near freezing. By far my favourite comment, by 'FossilDAWG', in response to a discussion of the possibility of megalodon adapting to life in the deep sea (including a change in diet from whales to something else) is, 'I think I'd rather believe them to be extinct, than to think they had evolved into a species of toothless jellyfish suckers.

Somehow, that seems like an ignominious fate for such a magnificent predator.'

The deepest parts of our oceans, which are 11 kilometres below the surface, are barely explored. But what we know about them is enough for scientists to be sure that a megalodon could not survive there. In fact, no fish or other vertebrate can do so, because the water pressure is so extreme that it prevents the proper formation of the proteins required to make a vertebrate body. The deepest any fish has been recorded at is about 8000 metres, a record held by the sluggish and gelatinous Marianas snailfish. The megalodon, which was warm-blooded and voracious, wouldn't stand a chance in the freezing, highly pressured Marianas Trench, where food is so scarce.

At lesser depths in the oceans, however, conditions are not so severe, and large vertebrates can flourish. Such regions, including the ocean's twilight zone, continue to yield surprises. The discovery in 1938 of the living coelacanth, up until then known only from 66-million-year-old fossils, created a sensation which to this day encourages amateur cryptozoologists the world over to wonder what else is out there. And they have been further encouraged by recent research that has removed one big obstacle to the possibility of the megalodon's survival in the ocean deep—a supposed lack of food.

In recent years scientists have learned a great deal about
the deep ocean by tagging large fish and marine mammals.
As a result, many species which were thought to be surface
dwellers are now known to dive really deep—all the way
to the Bathyal (or Midnight) Zone, some 1000–3000 metres
below the surface. Whale sharks, elephant seals, beaked
whales, tuna and swordfish all make the journey, and the
reason they do so is to feed. Scientists have discovered that
there's lots of food down there, packed so densely that Navy
radar operators in the 1940s found that their signal was
bouncing off a living layer of organisms, creating a 'false
bottom' on their screens. The hordes of fish and other
creatures that comprise this layer move up and down the
water column, feeding near the surface at night and seeking refuge in the abyss by day. Their vertical migration is
considered to be the largest migration undertaken by any
organisms anywhere on Earth.

One of the species that makes the journey—the spiny-
toothed bristlemouth—is estimated to be the most abundant vertebrate on the planet. They are 7.5 centimetres long
and there are quadrillions of them. Almost as abundant are
the similar-sized lanternfish, which have a high oil content
and thus provide excellent nutrition for predators. These
blizzards of fish, along with the countless planktonic life
forms that are their prey, are accompanied in their migrations by such giants as the muscular squid. The bounty is

so great that even great white sharks have been known to dive hundreds of metres down to feast, using warm water eddies to avoid suffering hypothermia.

The ocean's twilight and midnight zones continue to yield astonishing discoveries, including of gigantic sharks whose existence was not previously suspected, such as the megamouth shark, which was first seen on 15 November 1976. At up to 5.5 metres long and a tonne in weight, the megamouth is a true giant, and it seems astonishing that such a species could go unrecorded until so recently. Megamouth's most distinctive characteristic is its huge head, which seems outsized relative to the body. It is a poor swimmer, is soft and flabby and lacks the keels near the tail that are so characteristic of faster-moving sharks. Many images show the megamouth with haunting eyes, though strangely in other photographs the eyes are small and recessed, perhaps as a result of decomposition. Its skin varies in colour from blue to brown, with white margins on the rear of the fins. All individuals have a striking, silvery white upper lip.

Humanity's first encounter with a megamouth, in 1976, was a complete accident. A live individual became entangled in the sea-anchor of the US navy ship *AFB-14* about 65 kilometres north-east of Kahuku Island, Hawaii. When the shark came up from a depth of 165 metres, the captain realised that they had snagged something unusual, and he brought the body back to port, where biologists examined

it. The creature proved to be so distinctive that Leighton
Taylor and his colleagues, who were tasked with classifying
the beast, had to create a new genus for it. Subsequently,
many biologists consider that it should be placed in its own
family—a very high level of classification indeed—which
testifies to just how unusual the megamouth is. The discovery, hailed as one of the most sensational biological finds
of the 20th Century, alerted people to the existence of the
species, and today about 100 individual megamouth sharks
have been recorded.

Megamouths occur throughout much of the temperate
Pacific, Indian and Atlantic oceans. Like the whale shark,
it feeds on plankton. Its white lower lip may serve to attract
prey, which is then collected on finger-like gill rakers which
filter the water as the megamouth swims, enormous mouth
agape, through swarms of plankton. Megamouths seem to
follow the migrating plankton, spending most of their time
at depths of between 200 and 1000 metres. The distinctive,
tiny teeth of the megamouth are not used in feeding. They
have, however, proved useful in establishing the antiquity
of its lineage. A single fossil tooth found in Denmark and
belonging to an ancestral extinct species of megamouth
was recovered from 35-million-year-old marine sediments,
and fossil teeth belonging to the living species have been
found in 20-million-year-old rocks in Belgium. These

fossils tell us that the megamouth was a contemporary of the megalodon.

In 2010 scientists published a research paper that described how they had trawled up a completely unknown jet-black shark from the depths. In contrast to the megamouth, the new species was tiny—just 45 centimetres long. Named the ninja lantern shark, its most extraordinary characteristic is that it can glow in the dark. It has long, pointed teeth, but is so recently discovered that as yet we know almost nothing about its food preferences or other habits. It has been named *Etmopterus benchleyi*, honouring Peter Benchley, the author of the novel *Jaws*.

The discovery of megamouth—a hitherto unknown 5.5-metre-long shark in the deep ocean—has given new hope to the cryptozoologists that the megalodon lives on. Can we be certain no megalodons lurk in the ocean, they ask? I think so. If the megalodon was still extant, it would likely hunt where most of the food is, close to the surface. And surely it would still use coastal nurseries for its young, where it could be easily spotted. Besides, even the most elusive large sea creatures leave the occasional clue as to their presence. Every so often a giant squid, or a rotting body of the even larger colossal squid, washes up on a beach somewhere, or is captured on a deep-sea camera. Were it still extant, the megalodon surely would have left at least

a trace—a bite mark on unlucky prey, perhaps—or even
a fresh shiny tooth that might be trawled from the depths.

These lines of argument do little, I'll admit, to dissuade
the true believers who, in the deeper recesses of the internet,
continue to fervently discuss accounts of megalodon sightings. One close encounter supposedly occurred in 1918 near
Port Stephens, north of Sydney, when a group of stunned
commercial fishermen were so frightened by what they saw
that they were unable to return to the sea in the days following. The fishermen were in deep water off Broughton
Island, tending to their catch of crayfish, when a monster
approached and proceeded to snatch crayfish pot after
crayfish pot, taking 'mooring lines and all'. Those present
described the water 'boiling over' as the pale shark swam
by. Brimming with both excitement and fear, the fishermen
estimated the beast to have been between 35 and 90 metres
in length—even larger than the most monstrous megalodon, and at least four times the length of a blue whale.
The account, while clearly hyperbolic, may have been the
product of a rare sighting of an albino specimen of a whale
shark, a species known to use its cavernous mouth to suck
in hordes of fish through trawling nets. Or perhaps they
simply saw a very large great white shark that had become
tangled in their gear. Certainly, the energy and ferocity of
great whites can be such that they appear larger than they
in fact are.

A further sighting of a large shark, reputed by believers to be the megalodon, occurred in the 1960s, on the outer reaches of the Great Barrier Reef. Several sailors aboard their 26-metre-long yacht watched in awe as a colossal shark swam by. They said the shark was at least the length of their vessel, which has been taken as evidence by some cryptozoologists that this was a surviving megalodon. Another contender is the legendary 'black demon shark of Cortez', of which several sightings have been made off Mexico's Baja coast, intriguingly close to where fossils of the megalodon are frequently found. This behemoth is purported to be up to 18 metres long, with skin as black as midnight and jaws so large they could swallow a whale. Its body shape is said to be similar to that of the great white shark, but with an oversized tail.

The black demon shark of Cortez has been detailed in special episodes on both the Discovery Channel and the History Channel in the USA. In an attempt to attract it, producers for the Discovery Channel trailed large inflated whales behind their boat, while piping whale song into the ocean. Unsurprisingly the attempt was futile. Perhaps the black demon is another misidentified whale shark, or perhaps a very large great white. Or perhaps it is pure fantasy. The Discovery Channel, incidentally, has become an important source of information fuelling the idea that the megalodon lives on. Participants in internet forums focused

on the question of whether the megalodon survives tend to
quote Discovery as a trusted source. In 2014, during shark
week (an annual week-long TV special devoted to sharks by
Discovery), a program aired titled *Megalodon: The Monster
Shark Lives*. Both so-called scientists and eyewitnesses were
presented with evidence and accounts detailing supposed
encounters with the megalodon and asked to respond. This
episode garnered record ratings and went on to become the
highest-viewed episode aired during shark week of all time,
with almost five million viewers. Strangely, the scientists
who had been interviewed for the program were unable to
be traced, and records of some megalodon sightings men-
tioned on the program proved to be nothing but fantasy.
There is even evidence that Discovery may have doctored
a photograph (purportedly taken in 1942) shown on the
program. It depicts a giant dorsal fin and tail protruding
from the water next to two Nazi U-boats cruising off Cape
Town, South Africa. Discovery is for the most part known
for its informative shows on science, technology and nature,
making it all the more pertinent that at the closing cred-
its of the show, the program was divulged as a fiction—a
kind of mockumentary. Sadly, this was too little, too late to
enlighten those claiming that the megalodon lives.

   YouTube channels also abound with well-watched videos from engaging personalities who pose as experts on
the megalodon. Bill, an American man from 'billschannel',

has over 2.6 million subscribers on his 'Real or Fake' series. Viewers eagerly send in documentation of sightings of the megalodon, from the clearly doctored photos of a supposed specimen washed up on shore to those that are at least superficially more convincing, to be evaluated by Bill. One of the more persuasive videos sent in shows a large and blurry creature swimming past on the very edge of the frame. The footage was purportedly taken by the Brazilian coast-guard during a rescue operation. At 18 metres long, the creature is much too large to be a great white shark, and both the presence of a large dorsal fin and the way it moves its body from side to side while swimming refute the possibility it is a whale. After analysing the footage, however, Bill reveals it to be fake, made by none other than Discovery Channel! In 2015 the incoming president of the Discovery Channel Group, Rich Ross, said that regardless of how well these bogus shows have done for the company, it is just not right for Discovery Channel to continue to produce them.

In the 19th Century, the great British zoologist Alfred Russel Wallace mused, 'We live in a zoologically impoverished world, from which all the hugest, and fiercest, and strangest forms have recently disappeared.' The woolly mammoth, the sabre-tooth and the megalodon must be listed among these giants of past ages. There is something in their disappearance that has us keening at their loss, and even trying to somehow restore them. And so it is that scientists attempt to give rise to a living woolly mammoth through genetic manipulation. Others, without access to such tools, can only create an imagined, or merely hopeful world, within which such creatures live on. As I write the conclusion to this book, I take a moment to sit with one of my favourite fossil megalodon teeth. It's not a super-large tooth, but it is cream coloured with a beautiful pink tip, its root marked with myriad bullseye patterns. For me it is affirmation that the megalodon does indeed live on—if only in my imagination. I can't be sure whether my imagined beast truly resembles the creature that once lived and killed and ate on the high seas near my home. Only more science, and a whole lot more lucky discoveries, will reveal the megalodon in all its terrifying glory.

References

Chapter 2   *The Megalodon*

Aguilera, O. A. and Rodrigues De Aguilera, D., 'Giant-toothed White Sharks and Wide-toothed Mako (Lamnidae) from the Venezuela Neogene: Their role in the Caribbean, Shallow-water Fish Assemblage', *Caribbean Journal of Science*, Vol. 40.3, 368–82, 2004.

Aguilera, O. A., Garcia, L. and Cozzuol, M. A., 'Giant-toothed White Sharks and Cetacean Trophic Interaction from the Pliocene Caribbean Paraguaná Formation', *Paläontologische Zeitschrift*, Vol. 82.2, 204–08, 2008.

Cooper, J. A. *et al*, 'Body Dimensions of the Extinct Giant Shark *Otodus Megalodon*: A 2D Reconstruction', *Scientific Reports*, Vol. 10.1, Article No. 14596, 2020.

Ferrón H. G., 'Regional Endothermy as a Trigger for Gigantism in Some Extinct Macropredatory Sharks', *PLoS ONE*, Vol. 12.9, 2017.

Godfrey, S. J. and Altman, J., 'A Miocene Cetacean Vertebra Showing a Partially Healed Compression Fracture, the Result of Convulsions or Failed Predation by the Giant White Shark, *Carcharodon Megalodon*', Virginia Museum of Natural History, 2005.

Gottfried, M. D., 'Size and Skeletal Anatomy of the Giant "Megatooth" Shark *Carcharodon Megalodon*', in Klimley, P. A. and Ainley, D. G. (eds),

Great White Sharks: The Biology of Carcharodon Carcharias, Academic Press, Elsevier Inc., 1996.

Herraiz, J. L. *et al*, 'Use of Nursery Areas by the Extinct Megatooth Shark *Otodus Megalodon* (Chondrichthyes: Lamniformes)', *Biology Letters*, Vol. 16.11, 2020.

Kallal, R. J., Godfrey, S. J. and Ortner, D. J., 'Bone Reactions on a Pliocene Cetacean Rib Indicate Short-term Survival of Predation Event', *International Journal of Osteoarchaeology*, Vol. 22.3, 2012.

Kenshu S., Bonnan, M. F., Becker, M. A. and Griffiths, M. L., 'Ontogenetic Growth Pattern of the Extinct Megatooth Shark *Otodus Megalodon*—Implications for Its Reproductive Biology, Development, and Life Expectancy', *Historical Biology*, Vol. 33.12, 2021.

Perez, V., Leder, R. and Badaut, T., 'Body Length Macrophagous Lamniform Sharks (Carcharodon and Otodus) Derived from Associated Fossil Dentitions', *Palaeontologia Electronica*, Vol. 24.1, 2021.

Pimiento, C. and Balk, M. A., 'Body-size Trends of the Extinct Giant Shark *Carcharocles Megalodon*: A Deep-time Perspective on Marine Apex Predators', *Paleobiology*, Vol. 41.3, 2015.

Pimiento, C. *et al*, 'Ancient Nursery Area for the Extinct Giant Shark Megalodon from the Miocene of Panama', *PLoS ONE*, Vol. 5.5, 2010.

Shimada, K. *et al*, 'Revisiting Body Size Trends and Nursery Areas of the Neogene Megatooth Shark, *Otodus Megalodon* (Lamniformes: Otodontidae), Reveals Bergmann's Rule Possibly Enhanced Its Gigantism in Cooler Waters', *Historical Biology*, Vol. 35.2, 2023.

Shimada, K., Becker, M. A. and Griffiths, M. L., 'Body, Jaw, and Dentition Lengths of Macrophagous Lamniform Sharks, and Body Size Evolution in Lamniformes with Special Reference to 'Off-the-scale' Gigantism of the Megatooth Shark, *Otodus Megalodon*', *Historical Biology*, Vol. 33.1, 2020.

Wroe, S. *et al*, 'Three-dimensional Computer Analysis of White Shark Jaw Mechanics: How Hard Can a Great White bite?', *Journal of Zoology*, Vol. 276.4, 2008.

Uyeno, T., Sakamoto, O. and Sekine, H., 'Description of an Almost Complete Tooth Set of *Carcharodon Megalodon* from a Middle Miocene Bed in Saitama Prefecture, Japan', *Bulletin of the Saitama Museum of Natural History*, Vol. 7, 1989.

Herraiz, J. L. *et al*, 'Use of Nursery Areas by the Extinct Megatooth Shark *Otodus Megalodon* (Chondrichthyes: Lamniformes)', Vol. 16.11, 2020.

Chapter 3   *Origins: The Evolution of Sharks*

Long J. A. *et al*, 'First Shark from the Late Devonian (Frasnian) Gogo Formation, Western Australia Sheds New Light on the Development of Tessellated Calcified Cartilage', *PLoS ONE*, Vol. 10.6, 2015.

Bazzi, M. *et al*, 'Tooth Morphology Elucidates Shark Evolution across the End-Cretaceous Mass Extinction,' *PLoS Biology*, Vol. 19.8, 2021.

Fanti, F. *et al*, 'An Exceptionally Preserved Eocene Shark and the Rise of Modern Predator–Prey Interactions in the Coral Reef Food Web,' *Zoological Letters*, Vol. 2.1, 2016.

Frey, L. *et al*, 'The Early Elasmobranch *Phoebodus*: Phylogenetic Relationships, Ecomorphology and a New Time-scale for Shark Evolution', *Proceedings of the Royal Society B*, Vol. 286. 1912, 2019.

Jambura, P. L. *et al*, 'Micro-computed Tomography Imaging Reveals the Development of a Unique Tooth Mineralization Pattern in Mackerel Sharks (Chondrichthyes; Lamniformes) in Deep Time', *Scientific Reports*, Vol. 9. 9652, 2019.

Miller, R., Cloutier, R. and Turner, S., 'The Oldest Articulated Chondrichthyan from the Early Devonian Period', *Nature*, Vol. 425, 2003.

Perez, V. J. *et al*, 'The Transition between *Carcharocles Chubutensis* and *Carcharocles Megalodon* (Otodontidae, Chondrichthyes): Lateral Cusplet Loss through Time', *Journal of Vertebrate Paleontology*, Vol. 38.6, 2018.

Renz, A. J., Meyer, A. and Kuraku, S., 'Revealing Less Derived Nature of Cartilaginous Fish Genomes with Their Evolutionary Time Scale Inferred with Nuclear Genes', *PLoS ONE*, Vol. 8.6, 2013.

Stigall, A. L., 'Speciation Collapse and Invasive Species Dynamics during the Late Devonian "Mass Extinction"', *GSA Today*, Vol. 22.1, 2012.

Stumpf, S. *et al*, 'A Unique Hybodontiform Skeleton Provides Novel Insights into Mesozoic Chondrichthyan Life', *Papers in Palaeontology*, Vol. 7.3, 2021.

Gottfried M. D. and Fordyce R. E., 'An Associated Specimen of *Carcharodon Angustidens* (Chondrichthyes, Lamnidae) from the Late Oligocene of New Zealand, with Comments on *Carcharodon* Interrelationships', *Journal of Vertebrate Paleontology*, Vol. 21.4, 2001.

Chapter 4 *The Miocene: The Megalodon's Heyday*

Collareta, A., *et al*, 'A Well Preserved Skeleton of the Fossil Shark *Cosmopolitodus Hastalis* from the Late Miocene of Peru, Featuring Fish Remains as Fossilized Stomach Contents', *Rivista Italiana di Paleontologia e Stratigrafia*, Vol. 123.1, 2017.

Perez, V. J., Stephen J. G., and Chapman, P. F., 'Rare Evidence of Shark-on-Shark Trophic Interactions in the Fossil Record', *Acta Palaeontologica Polonica*, Vol. 66.4, 2021.

Pyenson, N. D. and Sponberg, S. N., 'Reconstructing Body Size in Extinct Crown Cetacea (Neoceti) Using Allometry, Phylogenetic Methods and Tests from the Fossil Record', *Journal of Mammalian Evolution*, Vol. 18.4, 2011.

The Fish Site, 'Young Tuna Abundance Influenced by Cannibalism', 2011, https://thefishsite.com/articles/young-tuna-abundance-influenced-by -cannibalism.

Kast, E. R. *et al*, 'Cenozoic Megatooth Sharks Occupied Extremely High Trophic Positions', *ScienceAdvances*, Vol. 8.25, 2022.

Chapter 5 *Extinction*

Boessenecker, R. W. *et al*, 'The Early Pliocene Extinction of the Mega-toothed Shark *Otodus Megalodon*: A View from the Eastern North Pacific', *PeerJ*. Vol. 7, 2019.

Neumann, A. N. *et al*, 'The Extinction of Iconic Megatoothed Shark *Otodus megalodon*: Preliminary Evidence from "Clumped" Isotope Thermometry', *AGU Fall Meeting Abstracts*, 2018.

Pimiento, C. and Clements, C. F., 'When Did *Carcharocles Megalodon* Become Extinct? A New Analysis of the Fossil Record', *PloS ONE*, Vol. 9.10, 2014.

Pimiento, C. *et al*, 'Geographical Distribution Patterns of *Carcharocles Megalodon* Over Time Reveal Clues about Extinction Mechanisms', *Journal of Biogeography*, Vol. 43.8, 2016.

Wellard, R., *et al*, 'Killer Whale (*Orcinus Orca*) Predation on Beaked Whales (*Mesoplodon* spp.) in the Bremer Sub-Basin, Western Australia', *PloS ONE*, Vol. 11.12, 2016.

McCormack, J. *et al*, 'Trophic Position of *Otodus Megalodon* and Great White Sharks through Time Revealed by Zinc Isotopes', *Nature Communications*, Vol. 13.2980, 2022.

Towner, A. V. *et al*, 'Fear at the Top: Killer Whale Predation Drives White Shark Absence at South Africa's Largest Aggregation Site', *African Journal of Marine Science*, Vol. 44.2, 2022.

Chapter 6   *Charms, Tools and Jewels*

Charpentier, V., Adnet, S. and Cappetta, H., 'The Tooth of a Giant Sea Creature *Otodus* (*Megaselachus*) in the Material Culture of Neolithic Maritime Hunter-gatherers at Sharbithat (Sultanate of Oman)', *International Journal of Osteoarchaeology*, Vol. 30.6, 2020.

De Borhegyi, S. F., 'Shark Teeth, Stingray Spines, and Shark Fishing in Ancient Mexico and Central America', *Southwestern Journal of Anthropology*, Vol. 17.3, 1961.

Flannery, T. F. *et al*, *Tree kangaroos: A Curious Natural History*, Reed, Australia, 1996, p. 28.

Gilson, S. P. and Lessa, A., 'Capture, Processing and Utilization of Sharks in Archaeological Context: Its Importance among Fisher-hunter-gatherers from Southern Brazil', *Journal of Archaeological Science: Reports*, Vol. 35.102693, 2021.

Gilson, Simon-Pierre, *et al*, 'Shark Teeth Used as Tools: An Experimental Archaeology Study', *Journal of Archaeological Science: Reports*, Vol. 35.102733, 2021.

Rich, T. H. and Darragh, T. A., 'The Strange Case of the Wandering Fossil', *Bulletin of the American Museum of Natural History*, Vol. 279.5567, 2003.

Tütken, T, *et al*, 'Strontium and Oxygen Isotope Analyses Reveal Late Cretaceous Shark Teeth in Iron Age Strata in the Southern Levant', *Frontiers in Ecology and Evolution*, Vol. 8, 2020.

Lowcry, D., Godfrey, S. J. and Eshelman, R., 'Integrated Geology, Palaeontology, and Archaeology: Native American Use of Fossil Shark Teeth in the Chesapeake Bay Region', *Archaeology of Eastern North America*, Vol. 39, 2011.

Crane, B., 'A Prehistoric Killer, Buried in Muck, *New Yorker*, 5 March 2017.

The Specimen from Pertosa Cave, on display in the Museo Speleo Archaeologico, Pertosa, Italy.

Hoare, C., 'Scientists Baffled by 80-million-year-old Shark Fossils Found in Jerusalem', *Express*, 18 July 2021.

Chapter 7   *The Sweating Teeth of Malta*

Davidson, J. P., 'Fish Tales: Attributing the First Illustration of a Fossil Shark Tooth to Richard Verstegan (1605) and Nicolas Steno (1667)', *Proceedings of the Academy of Natural Sciences of Philadelphia*, Vol. 150, 2000.

Zamitt-Maempel, G., 'Fossil Shark Teeth: A Mediaeval Safeguard Against Poisoning', *Melita Historico*, Vol. 6.4, 1975.

Chapter 8   *The Don of Megalodons*

Vito Bertucci. stsharksjaws.com

Association of Applied Paleontological Sciences, 'Vito M. Bertucci 1956–2004'.

Chapter 9   *Where the Beautiful Megs Lie*

Ehret, D. J., and Ebersole, J., 'Occurrence of the Megatoothed Sharks (Lamniformes: Otodontidae) in Alabama, USA.' *PeerJ*, Vol 2.e625, 2014.

'Children Find Rare Fossilised Tooth Belonging to Prehistoric Ocean Giant', Essex Wildlife Trust, 2019.

Renz, M., *Megalodon: Hunting the Hunter*, Paleopress, 2002.

Wood, T., 'Searching for Megateeth', *Richmond Hill Magazine*, April–May 2008.

Chapter 10   *Shark Eats Man*

Shark Attack Data, sharkattackdata.com

Porter, M., 'Plea to Remove Killer Shark Netting from Cronulla's Beaches', *Leader*, 24 May 2021.

'Shark Killer Lands $18,000 Fine', *Fishing World*, 13 February 2014.

'Brother of Shark Victim Pleads for Creature's Life', *NBC News*, Associated Press, 12 July 2004.

Zaw, Y., 'Surfer's Plea to End Shark Cull', *West Australian*, 7 February 2014.

Chapter 11 *Man Eats Shark*

Bent, T. and Bent, M., *Southern Arabia*, Smith, Elder & Co., London, 1900.

Yeomans, L., 'Evidence for Fishing with Remora across the World and Archaeological Evidence from Southeast Arabia: A Case Study in Human-Animal Relations', *International Journal of Historical Archaeology*, 2021.

Shark-fin Soup, *Wikipedia*

Herz, R., 'You Eat That?', *Wall Street Journal*, 17 March 2015, updated 28 January 2022.

Carwardine, M., 'What Shark Finning Is and Why It Is a Problem', *Discover Wildlife*, BBC Wildlife Magazine, undated.

'Sharks at Risk: Scientists Say EU Shark Finning Ban Ineffective and Call for Major Change', *Oceana*, 2013.

Chapter 12 *The Imaginary Meg*

Guimont, E., 'The Megalodon: A Monster of the New Mythology', *M/C Journal*, Vol. 24.5, 2021.

Tschernezky, W., 'Age of *Carcharodon Megalodon?*', *Nature*, Vol. 184, 1959.

Yahr, E., 'A Fake Shark Week Documentary about Megalodons Caused Controversy: Why Is *Discovery* Bringing It up Again?' *Washington Post*, 26 July 2018.

Pain, S. and *Knowable Magazine*, 'Marine Scientists Are Getting to the Bottom of Why Some Big Fish Dive Deep, Deep Down', *Inverse*, 13 June 2023.

Index